# MAX LUCADO

## LIFE LESSONS *from*

# GALATIANS

*Free in Christ*

PREPARED BY THE LIVINGSTONE CORPORATION

THOMAS NELSON
*Since 1798*

Published in Nashville, Tennessee, by Thomas Nelson. Thomas Nelson is a registered trademark of HarperCollins Christian Publishing, Inc.

Produced with the assistance of the Livingstone Corporation. Project staff include Jake Barton, Joel Bartlett, Andy Culbertson, Will Reaves, Mary Horner Collins, and Rachel Hawkins.

Editor: Len Woods

All Scripture quotations, unless otherwise indicated, are taken from The Holy Bible, New International Version®, NIV®. Copyright © 1973, 1978, 1984, 2011 by Biblica, Inc.™ Used by permission. All rights reserved worldwide.

Scripture quotations marked NKJV are taken from the New King James Version®. Copyright © 1982 by Thomas Nelson. Used by permission. All rights reserved.

Scripture quotations marked NCV are taken from The Holy Bible, New Century Version (New International Version). Copyright ©1987, 1988, 1991 by Word Publishing. All rights reserved.

Scripture quotations marked TLB are taken from The Living Bible, copyright ©1971 by Tyndale House Foundation. Used by permission of Tyndale House Publishers Inc., Carol Stream, Illinois 60188. All rights reserved.

Material for the "Inspiration" sections taken from the following books:

*And the Angels Were Silent.* Copyright © 2004 by Max Lucado. Thomas Nelson, a registered trademark of HarperCollins Christian Publishing, Inc., Nashville, Tennessee.

*Anxious for Nothing.* Copyright © 2017 by Max Lucado. Thomas Nelson, a registered trademark of HarperCollins Christian Publishing, Inc., Nashville, Tennessee.

*Come Thirsty.* Copyright © 2004 by Max Lucado. Thomas Nelson, a registered trademark of HarperCollins Christian Publishing, Inc., Nashville, Tennessee.

*Cure for the Common Life.* Copyright © 2005 by Max Lucado. Thomas Nelson, a registered trademark of HarperCollins Christian Publishing, Inc., Nashville, Tennessee.

*A Gentle Thunder.* Copyright © 1995 by Max Lucado. Thomas Nelson, a registered trademark of HarperCollins Christian Publishing, Inc., Nashville, Tennessee.

*Grace.* Copyright © 2012 by Max Lucado. Thomas Nelson, a registered trademark of HarperCollins Christian Publishing, Inc., Nashville, Tennessee.

*In the Grip of Grace.* Copyright © 1996 by Max Lucado. Thomas Nelson, a registered trademark of HarperCollins Christian Publishing, Inc., Nashville, Tennessee.

*Just Like Jesus.* Copyright © 1998 by Max Lucado. Thomas Nelson, a registered trademark of HarperCollins Christian Publishing, Inc., Nashville, Tennessee.

*A Love Worth Giving.* Copyright © 2002 by Max Lucado. Thomas Nelson, a registered trademark of HarperCollins Christian Publishing, Inc., Nashville, Tennessee.

*Outlive Your Life.* Copyright © 2010 by Max Lucado. Thomas Nelson, a registered trademark of HarperCollins Christian Publishing, Inc., Nashville, Tennessee

*When God Whispers Your Name.* Copyright © 1999 by Max Lucado. Thomas Nelson, a registered trademark of HarperCollins Christian Publishing, Inc., Nashville, Tennessee.

Thomas Nelson titles may be purchased in bulk for educational, business, fundraising, or sales promotional use. For information, please e-mail SpecialMarkets@ThomasNelson.com.

ISBN 978-0-310-08646-8

**First Printing May 2018 / Printed in the United States of America**

# CONTENTS

# HOW TO STUDY THE BIBLE

The Bible is a peculiar book. Words crafted in another language. Deeds done in a distant era. Events recorded in a far-off land. Counsel offered to a foreign people. It is a peculiar book.

It's surprising that anyone reads it. It's too old. Some of its writings date back 5,000 years. It's too bizarre. The book speaks of incredible floods, fires, earthquakes, and people with supernatural abilities. It's too radical. The Bible calls for undying devotion to a carpenter who called himself God's Son.

Logic says this book shouldn't survive. Too old, too bizarre, too radical.

The Bible has been banned, burned, scoffed, and ridiculed. Scholars have mocked it as foolish. Kings have branded it as illegal. A thousand times over the grave has been dug and the dirge has begun, but somehow the Bible never stays in the grave. Not only has it survived, but it has also thrived. It is the single most popular book in all of history. It has been the bestselling book in the world for years!

There is no way on earth to explain it. Which perhaps is the only explanation. For the Bible's durability is not found on *earth* but in *heaven*. The millions who have tested its claims and claimed its promises know there is but one answer: the Bible is God's book and God's voice.

As you read it, you would be wise to give some thought to two questions: *What is the purpose of the Bible?* and *How do I study the Bible?* Time spent reflecting on these two issues will greatly enhance your Bible study.

What is the purpose of the Bible?

Let the Bible itself answer that question: *"From infancy you have known the Holy Scriptures, which are able to make you wise for salvation through faith in Christ Jesus"* (2 Timothy 3:15).

The purpose of the Bible? Salvation. God's highest passion is to get his children home. His book, the Bible, describes his plan of salvation. The purpose of the Bible is to proclaim God's plan and passion to save his children.

This is the reason why this book has endured through the centuries. It dares to tackle the toughest questions about life: *Where do I go after I die? Is there a God? What do I do with my fears?* The Bible is the treasure map that leads to God's highest treasure—eternal life.

But how do you study the Bible? Countless copies of Scripture sit unread on bookshelves and nightstands simply because people don't know how to read it. What can you do to make the Bible real in your life?

The clearest answer is found in the words of Jesus: *"Ask and it will be given to you; seek and you will find; knock and the door will be opened to you"* (Matthew 7:7).

The first step in understanding the Bible is asking God to help you. You should read it prayerfully. If anyone understands God's Word, it is because of God and not the reader.

*"The Advocate, the Holy Spirit, whom the Father will send in my name, will teach you all things and will remind you of everything I have said to you"* (John 14:26).

Before reading the Bible, pray and invite God to speak to you. Don't go to Scripture looking for your idea, but go searching for his.

Not only should you read the Bible prayerfully, but you should also read it carefully. *"Seek and you will find"* is the pledge. The Bible is not a newspaper to be skimmed but rather a mine to be quarried. *"If you look for it as for silver and search for it as for hidden treasure, then you will understand the fear of the LORD and find the knowledge of God"* (Proverbs 2:4–5).

Any worthy find requires effort. The Bible is no exception. To understand the Bible, you don't have to be brilliant, but you must be willing to roll up your sleeves and search.

*"Do your best to present yourself to God as one approved, a worker who does not need to be ashamed and who correctly handles the word of truth"* (2 Timothy 2:15).

Here's a practical point. Study the Bible a bit at a time. Hunger is not satisfied by eating twenty-one meals in one sitting once a week. The body needs a steady diet to remain strong. So does the soul. When God sent food to his people in the wilderness, he didn't provide loaves already made. Instead, he sent them manna in the shape of *"thin flakes like frost on the ground"* (Exodus 16:14).

God gave manna in limited portions.

God sends spiritual food the same way. He opens the heavens with just enough nutrients for today's hunger. He provides *"a rule for this, a rule for that; a little here, a little there"* (Isaiah 28:10).

Don't be discouraged if your reading reaps a small harvest. Some days a lesser portion is all that is needed. What is important is to search every day for that day's message. A steady diet of God's Word over a lifetime builds a healthy soul and mind.

It's much like the little girl who returned from her first day at school feeling a bit dejected. Her mom asked, "Did you learn anything?"

"Apparently not enough," the girl responded. "I have to go back tomorrow, and the next day, and the next . . . "

Such is the case with learning. And such is the case with Bible study. Understanding comes little by little over a lifetime.

There is a third step in understanding the Bible. After the asking and seeking comes the knocking. After you ask and search, *"knock and the door will be opened to you"* (Matthew 7:7).

To knock is to stand at God's door. To make yourself available. To climb the steps, cross the porch, stand at the doorway, and volunteer. Knocking goes beyond the realm of thinking and into the realm of acting.

To knock is to ask, *What can I do? How can I obey? Where can I go?*

It's one thing to know what to do. It's another to do it. But for those who do it—those who choose to obey—a special reward awaits them.

*"Whoever looks intently into the perfect law that gives freedom, and continues in it—not forgetting what they have heard, but doing it—they will be blessed in what they do"* (James 1:25).

What a promise. Blessings come to those who do what they read in God's Word! It's the same with medicine. If you only read the label but ignore the pills, it won't help. It's the same with food. If you only read the recipe but never cook, you won't be fed. And it's the same with the Bible. If you only read the words but never obey, you'll never know the joy God has promised.

Ask. Search. Knock. Simple, isn't it? So why don't you give it a try? If you do, you'll see why the Bible is the most remarkable book in history.

# INTRODUCTION TO
## *The Book of Galatians*

The Emancipation Proclamation was ready to be signed. The papers were complete. All that was lacking was the signature of the president. But Abraham Lincoln was not ready. He had spent the morning at a reception and his hand was swollen from greeting visitors.

"Let me wait until my hand is better," he reportedly requested. "I don't want my signature to be shaky. I want people to know I set the slaves free in confidence."

Galatians states that Christ did the same for us. "He set the slaves free in confidence." No hesitation. No reservation. No reluctance. No exceptions.

The book of Galatians is the Emancipation Proclamation for the church. Written by one who had known slavery, it declares and defines Christian liberty. Paul wrote it to refute the devilish idea that salvation is based on adherence to a religious code.

Many of the early Christians were Jewish Christians who were accustomed to following the Law. Though they had accepted the gift of grace offered by Christ on the cross, some were falling away and substituting human effort for God's gift. Paul recognized this for what it was: legalism.

Everywhere the gospel has been preached, there have been those who contend it is too good to be true. Some argue it's not enough to be saved by faith; we must earn God's approval (legalism). Some teach we earn God's favor by what we know (intellectualism). Others insist we are saved by what we do (moralism). Still others claim that salvation is determined by what we feel (emotionalism).

However you package it, Paul contests, legalism is heresy. Salvation comes only through the cross—no additions, no alterations.

We are free in Christ. "It is for freedom that Christ has set us free. Stand firm, then, and do not let yourselves be burdened again by a yoke of slavery" (Galatians 5:1). Galatians is a document of freedom. As you read, note the confidence of the writer. His hand doesn't shake, his conviction doesn't waver, his belief doesn't falter.

Neither should ours.

## AUTHOR AND DATE

Paul, who persecuted the early church before his life was radically altered by meeting the risen Jesus on the road to Damascus (see Acts 9:1–31). Paul and Barnabas established churches in several cities in the Roman province of Galatia (the south-central part of modern-day Turkey) during their first missionary journey c. AD 47 (see Acts 13–14). It is likely Paul wrote the letter of Galatians to the congregations in this region shortly after this journey but before the Jerusalem Council took place c. AD 48 or 49. If this date of composition is correct, it would make Galatians the earliest of Paul's existing letters. It is not known where Paul was based when he composed this letter, but it is possible that he wrote it from Jerusalem.

## SITUATION

After Paul returned from his first missionary journey, he received reports that teachers preaching "a different gospel" had infiltrated the Galatian churches and were "trying to pervert the gospel of Christ" (Galatians 1:6–7). These teachers were proclaiming that if the people wanted to receive salvation from Christ, they also had to follow all the laws of Moses, observe the Jewish customs, and in effect become "practical Jews" (see Acts 15:1–5). So many of the Galatians were being persuaded by this argument that Paul was compelled to meet the threat head-on by writing a no-holds-barred letter that showed them the error of this way of thinking. For Paul, only faith in the saving work of Jesus was required for salvation, and he wanted the Galatian believers to remember the true gospel of grace that he had shared with them.

## KEY THEMES

- Salvation comes by grace, not works.
- We should bear the fruit of the Holy Spirit in our lives.
- We will reap in life what we have sown in life.

## KEY VERSE

*Are you so foolish? After beginning by means of the Spirit, are you now trying to finish by means of the flesh? (Galatians 3:3).*

## CONTENTS

I. The Gospel of Grace (1:1–2:21)
II. What to Believe About Grace (3:1–4:31)
III. How to Live in Grace (5:1–6:18)

# LEAVING GRACE?

*I am astonished that you are so quickly
deserting the one who called you to live in the
grace of Christ and are turning to a different
gospel—which is really no gospel at all.*

# REFLECTION

Most people do not enjoy confrontation. Few go through life looking to pick a fight. And yet, conflict is an unavoidable fact of life. What is your typical course of action when you find you have to speak hard truths to a friend, neighbor, or colleague?

_____

_____

_____

_____

_____

_____

_____

_____

_____

_____

# SITUATION

During Paul's first missionary journey, he and Barnabas planted a number of churches in the Roman province of Galatia. It was a successful trip, but upon his return, he learned that other teachers had arrived in the region and were preaching a different gospel—one based on salvation through works and adhering to Jewish laws and customs. Paul was troubled to hear that many people in the churches he had founded were being easily swayed by this idea that salvation was *not* through grace alone. In response, Paul forgoes his words of "thanksgiving and praise" for the believers so common in his letters and gets straight to the heart of his concerns.

# OBSERVATION

*Read Galatians 1:1–10 from the New International*
*Version or the New King James Version.*

## NEW INTERNATIONAL VERSION

[1] Paul, an apostle—sent not from men nor by a man, but by Jesus Christ and God the Father, who raised him from the dead— [2] and all the brothers and sisters with me,

To the churches in Galatia:

[3] Grace and peace to you from God our Father and the Lord Jesus Christ, [4] who gave himself for our sins to rescue us from the present evil age, according to the will of our God and Father, [5] to whom be glory for ever and ever. Amen.

[6] I am astonished that you are so quickly deserting the one who called you to live in the grace of Christ and are turning to a different gospel— [7] which is really no gospel at all. Evidently some people are throwing you into confusion and are trying to pervert the gospel of Christ.[8] But even if we or an angel from heaven should preach a gospel other than the one we preached to you, let them be under God's curse! [9] As we have already said, so now I say again: If anybody is preaching to you a gospel other than what you accepted, let them be under God's curse!

[10] Am I now trying to win the approval of human beings, or of God? Or am I trying to please people? If I were still trying to please people, I would not be a servant of Christ.

## NEW KING JAMES VERSION

[1] Paul, an apostle (not from men nor through man, but through Jesus Christ and God the Father who raised Him from the dead), [2] and all the brethren who are with me,

To the churches of Galatia:

[3] Grace to you and peace from God the Father and our Lord Jesus Christ, [4] who gave Himself for our sins, that He might deliver us from

this present evil age, according to the will of our God and Father, ⁵ to whom be glory forever and ever. Amen.

⁶ I marvel that you are turning away so soon from Him who called you in the grace of Christ, to a different gospel, ⁷ which is not another; but there are some who trouble you and want to pervert the gospel of Christ. ⁸ But even if we, or an angel from heaven, preach any other gospel to you than what we have preached to you, let him be accursed. ⁹ As we have said before, so now I say again, if anyone preaches any other gospel to you than what you have received, let him be accursed.

¹⁰ For do I now persuade men, or God? Or do I seek to please men? For if I still pleased men, I would not be a bondservant of Christ.

# EXPLORATION

**1.** The first sentences of Paul's letter to the Galatians have an abrupt and somber feel. Why do you think Paul chose to open in this manner?

**2.** Paul begins by presenting his "credentials" as an apostle. Why do you think he felt the need to do this? When is such an action valid or invalid?

**3.** What reason does Paul give for being "astonished" (verse 6)?

**4.** Why is the "new gospel" the Galatians are embracing *not* good news?

_____

_____

_____

**5.** The word "curse" Paul uses in verses 8 and 9 means "eternally condemned." What does this suggest about tinkering with the gospel or altering Christ's message?

_____

_____

_____

**6.** What is the "simple gospel" (see also 1 Corinthians 15:1–4)?

_____

_____

# INSPIRATION

*What is the work God wants us to do? Pray more? Give more? Study? Travel? Memorize the Torah? What is the work he wants?*

Sly is this scheme of Satan. Rather than lead us away from grace, he causes us to question grace or to earn it . . . and in the end we never even know it.

What is it, then, that God wants us to do? What is the work he seeks? Just believe. Believe the one he sent. "The work of God is this: to believe in the one he has sent" (John 6:29).

Someone is reading this and shaking his or her head and asking, "Are you saying it is possible to go to heaven with no good works?" The answer is *no*. Good works are a requirement. Someone else is reading and asking, "Are you saying it is possible to go to heaven without good character?" My answer again is *no*. Good character is also required. In order to enter heaven, one must have good works and good character.

But, alas, there is the problem. You have neither.

Oh, you've done some nice things in your life. But you do not have enough good works to go to heaven regardless of your sacrifice. No matter how noble your gifts, they are not enough to get you into heaven.

Nor do you have enough character to go to heaven. Please don't be offended. (Then again, be offended, if necessary.) You're probably a very decent person. But decency isn't enough. Those who see God are not the decent; they are the holy. "Without holiness no one will see the Lord" (Hebrews 12:14).

You may be decent. You may pay taxes and kiss your kids and sleep with a clean conscience. But apart from Christ you aren't holy. So how can you go to heaven?

Only believe.

Accept the work already done, the work of Jesus on the cross. Only believe . . .

It's that simple? It's that simple. It's that easy? There was nothing easy at all about it. The cross was heavy, the blood was real, and the price was extravagant. It would have bankrupted you or me, so Jesus paid it for us. Call it simple. Call it a gift. But don't call it easy.

Call it what it is. Call it grace. (From *A Gentle Thunder* by Max Lucado.)

# REACTION

**7.** Why do you think it is so hard for people to grasp the concept of grace?

_____

_____

_____

_____

**8.** What are some things (other than Christ) that Christians tend to rely on to try to establish their approval in God's sight?

**9.** How would you answer the person who read this passage and said, "I don't get why Paul is so upset over a few theological semantics?"

**10.** When you look at your church, do any trends "astonish" you or cause you to "marvel" (in a negative sense)?

**11.** Is the gospel message you share with others marked by radical and risky-sounding grace? Why or why not?

**12.** How will you respond the next time you hear someone share a distorted version of the gospel?

_____

_____

_____

_____

_____

_____

_____

# LIFE LESSONS

Grace is what sets Christianity apart from every religion in the world. God offers his unearnable salvation, forgiveness, and eternal life not as a *reward* but as a free *gift*. Nothing—absolutely *nothing*—is required on our part except to believe. There is no fine print and no strings attached. When we trust in what Christ has done and rely solely on his promises, all the treasures of heaven are ours. It doesn't matter how miserably we've failed in the past. It's irrelevant how messed up our lives are right now. Grace is true and certain no matter what we might do or fail to do in the future. It sounds too good to be true . . . but that, in a nutshell, is the simple gospel. The only question is this: *Have you received Christ's remarkable gift?*

# DEVOTION

*Father, thank you for the gospel. We could never earn your favor, but we can be recipients of your grace. We can enjoy all your blessings simply by trusting in Christ as our all-sufficient Savior. Help us to live this message. Help us to show it by our lives and share it with our lips.*

# JOURNALING

When were you first struck by the "free" nature of the gospel—that faith, not works, is the doorway to peace with God?

# FOR FURTHER READING

To complete the book of Galatians during this twelve-part study, read Galatians 1:1–10. For more Bible passages on the gospel of grace, read Acts 15:6–21; Romans 3:21–24; 1 Corinthians 15:1–11; Ephesians 2:8–9; and Titus 3:4–7.

# DEFENDING THE GOSPEL

*But I make known to you, brethren, that the gospel*
*which was preached by me is not according to man. . . .*
*It came through the revelation of Jesus Christ.*
GALATIANS 1:11–12 NKJV

# REFLECTION

In one sense, life is all about our interaction with God. Some of us have run from him in the past. Others of us are finding our way back to him. What is your unique faith story?

_____

_____

_____

_____

_____

# SITUATION

Now that Paul has gotten his readers' attention with his opening remarks, he begins to set out the case for the true gospel of grace that he presented when he was with them. To do this, he will draw on examples from his own past in Judaism and show how the process of how he went from being a fierce persecutor of the church to a set-apart minister to the Gentiles (non-Jews). Paul rehearses these particular incidents to show that he did not receive this gospel of grace from any person, but in truth received it directly from God.

# OBSERVATION

*Read Galatians 1:11–24 from the New International Version or the New King James Version.*

NEW INTERNATIONAL VERSION

[11] I want you to know, brothers and sisters, that the gospel I preached is not of human origin. [12] I did not receive it from any man, nor was I taught it; rather, I received it by revelation from Jesus Christ.

[13] For you have heard of my previous way of life in Judaism, how intensely I persecuted the church of God and tried to destroy it. [14] I was advancing in Judaism beyond many of my own age among my people and was extremely zealous for the traditions of my fathers. [15] But when God, who set me apart from my mother's womb and called me by his grace, was pleased [16] to reveal his Son in me so that I might preach him among the Gentiles, my immediate response was not to consult any human being. [17] I did not go up to Jerusalem to see those who were apostles before I was, but I went into Arabia. Later I returned to Damascus.

[18] Then after three years, I went up to Jerusalem to get acquainted with Cephas and stayed with him fifteen days. [19] I saw none of the other apostles—only James, the Lord's brother. [20] I assure you before God that what I am writing you is no lie.

[21] Then I went to Syria and Cilicia. [22] I was personally unknown to the churches of Judea that are in Christ. [23] They only heard the report: "The man who formerly persecuted us is now preaching the faith he once tried to destroy." [24] And they praised God because of me.

## NEW KING JAMES VERSION

[11] But I make known to you, brethren, that the gospel which was preached by me is not according to man. [12] For I neither received it from man, nor was I taught it, but it came through the revelation of Jesus Christ.

[13] For you have heard of my former conduct in Judaism, how I persecuted the church of God beyond measure and tried to destroy it. [14] And I advanced in Judaism beyond many of my contemporaries in my own nation, being more exceedingly zealous for the traditions of my fathers.

[15] But when it pleased God, who separated me from my mother's womb and called me through His grace, [16] to reveal His Son in me, that I might preach Him among the Gentiles, I did not immediately confer with flesh and blood, [17] nor did I go up to Jerusalem to those who were apostles before me; but I went to Arabia, and returned again to Damascus.

[18] Then after three years I went up to Jerusalem to see Peter, and remained with him fifteen days. [19] But I saw none of the other apostles

except James, the Lord's brother. [20] (Now concerning the things which I write to you, indeed, before God, I do not lie.)

[21] Afterward I went into the regions of Syria and Cilicia. [22] And I was unknown by face to the churches of Judea which were in Christ. [23] But they were hearing only, "He who formerly persecuted us now preaches the faith which he once tried to destroy." [24] And they glorified God in me.

# EXPLORATION

**1.** How does Paul describe the gospel that he preached to the Galatian believers?

_____

_____

_____

_____

**2.** Why was Paul an unlikely candidate for becoming a Christian—much less God's appointed missionary to the Gentiles (see Acts 9:1–20)?

_____

_____

_____

**3.** Why does Paul make such a big deal about not getting advice or help from any person (or persons) after his conversion?

_____

_____

_____

**4.** What does Paul's testimony reveal about God's patience and mercy?

_____

_____

_____

**5.** When did Christ first become real to you—more than just a name or an idea?

_____

_____

_____

**6.** Why do you think people get so fanatical about religion? How can you tell when zeal and passion have cross over the line into fanaticism?

_____

_____

# INSPIRATION

Guilt sucks the life out of our souls. Grace restores it. The apostle Paul clung to this grace. To the same degree that he believed in God's sovereignty, he relied on God's mercy.

No one had more reason to feel the burden of guilt than Paul did. He had orchestrated the deaths of Christians. He was an ancient version of a terrorist, taking believers into custody and then spilling their blood. "Saul began to destroy the church. Going from house to house, he dragged off both men and women and put them in prison" (Acts 8:3).

In addition, he was a legalist to the core. Before he knew Christ, Paul had spent a lifetime trying to save himself. His salvation depended on his perfection, on his performance. "If someone else thinks they have reasons to put confidence in the flesh, I have more: circumcised on the eighth day, of the people of Israel, of the tribe of Benjamin, a Hebrew of Hebrews; in regard to the law, a Pharisee; as for zeal, persecuting the church; as for righteousness based on the law, faultless" (Philippians 3:4–6).

Paul had blood on his hands and religious diplomas on his wall. But then came the Damascus road moment. Jesus appeared. Once Paul saw Jesus, he couldn't see anymore. He couldn't see value in his résumé anymore. He couldn't see merit in his merits or worth in his good works anymore. He couldn't see reasons to boast about anything he had done anymore. And he couldn't see any option except to spend the rest of his life talking less about himself and more about Jesus. (From *Anxious for Nothing* by Max Lucado.)

# REACTION

**7.** What situations in your own life are proof that God doesn't give up on his children?

_____

_____

_____

**8.** What features of the Christian faith indicate it obviously wasn't fabricated by humans?

_____

_____

**9.** How zealous are you? If you've lost your passion for Christ, how can you get it back?

_____

_____

_____

**10.** Scholars believe Paul spent his time in Arabia in study, reflection, and preparation for the message he would share. How do you find time for reflection in the midst of your busy life?

_____

_____

_____

**11.** Paul emphasizes how his experience with God was direct and not mediated through other people. How much of your knowledge of God is based on first-person experience?

**12.** Paul's conversion resulted in a dramatic transformation that had everyone buzzing. What have been the most significant changes in your life since you met Christ?

# LIFE LESSONS

It's often said, "The Lord works in mysterious ways." How true. Start with the gospel of grace. Are we to believe God offers enemies of the gospel unconditional pardon and adoption into his family? Or that heaven's most glorious riches are lavished on the least deserving? It all reads like a fairy tale. And it gets even wilder. God announces his intention to partner with the likes of *us* so others can experience his love and grace. He could use angels or employ supernatural means, but instead he uses us. And what do we do? Mostly, we stumble and fall and fail. Yet the Lord never gives up on us and never aborts his plan. He works in us, and through us, despite us. The villains become the heroes. What a mystery! What a miracle! What a God we serve!

# DEVOTION

*Father, you amaze us. Thank you for the beauty and power of the gospel that you have given to us. We open our hearts to you today and invite you to work through us. Transform us. Make our lives a continual tribute to your goodness and grace.*

# JOURNALING

How do you react when you consider the type of grace that God is offering to you today?

_____

_____

_____

_____

_____

_____

_____

_____

_____

_____

_____

_____

# FOR FURTHER READING

To complete the book of Galatians during this twelve-part study, read Galatians 1:11–24. For more Bible passages on zeal, read Psalm 119:137–144; John 2:13–17; 4:34–38; Acts 18:24–28; Romans 10:1–4; 1 Corinthians 9:19–23; and 2 Timothy 1:6–12.

# RIGHT WITH GOD

*I do not set aside the grace of God, for if
righteousness could be gained through
the law, Christ died for nothing!*
GALATIANS 2:21

# REFLECTION

Just about every religious community or church group has its own particular code of conduct. What were some of the activities—both prescribed and prohibited—by the spiritual community in which you grew up?

_____

_____

_____

_____

_____

_____

_____

_____

_____

_____

_____

_____

# SITUATION

Paul continues to relate his testimony in this portion of his letter to show how the "pillars" of the Jerusalem church—James, Peter, and John—not only approved of him sharing the gospel with the Gentiles but also did not require the new converts to adopt Jewish practices. In fact, the only requirement he was given was to "remember the poor" (Galatians 2:10), which Paul was more than eager to do. However, Paul then relates how the disciple Peter created confusion in Antioch by showing favoritism to the Jewish believers. Paul was willing to confront and correct even Peter on this point to reiterate only Jesus can make us right with God.

# OBSERVATION

*Read Galatians 2:1–21 from the New International*
*Version or the New King James Version.*

NEW INTERNATIONAL VERSION

[1] Then after fourteen years, I went up again to Jerusalem, this time with Barnabas. I took Titus along also. [2] I went in response to a revelation and, meeting privately with those esteemed as leaders, I presented to them the gospel that I preach among the Gentiles. I wanted to be sure I was not running and had not been running my race in vain. [3] Yet not even Titus, who was with me, was compelled to be circumcised, even though he was a Greek. [4] This matter arose because some false believers had infiltrated our ranks to spy on the freedom we have in Christ Jesus and to make us slaves. [5] We did not give in to them for a moment, so that the truth of the gospel might be preserved for you.

[6] As for those who were held in high esteem—whatever they were makes no difference to me; God does not show favoritism—they added nothing to my message. [7] On the contrary, they recognized that I had been entrusted with the task of preaching the gospel to the uncircumcised, just as Peter had been to the circumcised. [8] For God, who was at work in Peter as an apostle to the circumcised, was also at work in me as an apostle to the Gentiles. [9] James, Cephas and John, those esteemed as pillars, gave me and Barnabas the right hand of fellowship when they recognized the grace given to me. They agreed that we should go to the Gentiles, and they to the circumcised. [10] All they asked was that we should continue to remember the poor, the very thing I had been eager to do all along.

[11] When Cephas came to Antioch, I opposed him to his face, because he stood condemned. [12] For before certain men came from James, he used to eat with the Gentiles. But when they arrived, he began to draw back and separate himself from the Gentiles because he was afraid of those who belonged to the circumcision group. [13] The other Jews joined him in his hypocrisy, so that by their hypocrisy even Barnabas was led astray.

[14] When I saw that they were not acting in line with the truth of the gospel, I said to Cephas in front of them all, "You are a Jew, yet you live like a Gentile and not like a Jew. How is it, then, that you force Gentiles to follow Jewish customs?

[15] "We who are Jews by birth and not sinful Gentiles [16] know that a person is not justified by the works of the law, but by faith in Jesus Christ. So we, too, have put our faith in Christ Jesus that we may be justified by faith in Christ and not by the works of the law, because by the works of the law no one will be justified.

[17] "But if, in seeking to be justified in Christ, we Jews find ourselves also among the sinners, doesn't that mean that Christ promotes sin? Absolutely not! [18] If I rebuild what I destroyed, then I really would be a lawbreaker.

[19] "For through the law I died to the law so that I might live for God. [20] I have been crucified with Christ and I no longer live, but Christ lives in me. The life I now live in the body, I live by faith in the Son of God, who loved me and gave himself for me. [21] I do not set aside the grace of God, for if righteousness could be gained through the law, Christ died for nothing!"

## New King James Version

[1] Then after fourteen years I went up again to Jerusalem with Barnabas, and also took Titus with me. [2] And I went up by revelation, and communicated to them that gospel which I preach among the Gentiles, but privately to those who were of reputation, lest by any means I might run, or had run, in vain. [3] Yet not even Titus who was with me, being a Greek, was compelled to be circumcised. [4] And this occurred because of false brethren secretly brought in (who came in by stealth to spy out our liberty which we have in Christ Jesus, that they might bring us into bondage), [5] to whom we did not yield submission even for an hour, that the truth of the gospel might continue with you.

[6] But from those who seemed to be something—whatever they were, it makes no difference to me; God shows personal favoritism to no

man—for those who seemed to be something added nothing to me. [7] But on the contrary, when they saw that the gospel for the uncircumcised had been committed to me, as the gospel for the circumcised was to Peter [8] (for He who worked effectively in Peter for the apostleship to the circumcised also worked effectively in me toward the Gentiles), [9] and when James, Cephas, and John, who seemed to be pillars, perceived the grace that had been given to me, they gave me and Barnabas the right hand of fellowship, that we should go to the Gentiles and they to the circumcised. [10] They desired only that we should remember the poor, the very thing which I also was eager to do.

[11] Now when Peter had come to Antioch, I withstood him to his face, because he was to be blamed; [12] for before certain men came from James, he would eat with the Gentiles; but when they came, he withdrew and separated himself, fearing those who were of the circumcision. [13] And the rest of the Jews also played the hypocrite with him, so that even Barnabas was carried away with their hypocrisy.

[14] But when I saw that they were not straightforward about the truth of the gospel, I said to Peter before them all, "If you, being a Jew, live in the manner of Gentiles and not as the Jews, why do you compel Gentiles to live as Jews? [15] We who are Jews by nature, and not sinners of the Gentiles, [16] knowing that a man is not justified by the works of the law but by faith in Jesus Christ, even we have believed in Christ Jesus, that we might be justified by faith in Christ and not by the works of the law; for by the works of the law no flesh shall be justified.

[17] "But if, while we seek to be justified by Christ, we ourselves also are found sinners, is Christ therefore a minister of sin? Certainly not! [18] For if I build again those things which I destroyed, I make myself a transgressor. [19] For I through the law died to the law that I might live to God. [20] I have been crucified with Christ; it is no longer I who live, but Christ lives in me; and the life which I now live in the flesh I live by faith in the Son of God, who loved me and gave Himself for me. [21] I do not set aside the grace of God; for if righteousness comes through the law, then Christ died in vain."

# EXPLORATION

**1.** How does Paul say he approached the leaders in the Jerusalem church with his plan to preach the gospel to the Gentiles? How did they react?

**2.** What was Peter doing that warranted Paul's accusing him of hypocrisy?

**3.** What are some similar ways modern believers are guilty of presenting a distorted picture of the gospel of grace?

**4.** When should a Christian confront another Christian privately? When should such disagreements be handled publicly?

**5.** How would you define the word *justified* (which is found three times in verse 16)?

**6.** There have always been those who feel too much emphasis on grace encourages people to believe they can live however they want. Is this a valid concern? Why or why not?

_____

_____

_____

_____

# INSPIRATION

People are prone to pecking orders. We love the high horse. The boy over the girl or girl over boy. The affluent over the destitute. The educated over the dropout. The old-timer over the newcomer. The Jew over the Gentile.

An impassable gulf yawned between Jews and Gentiles in the days of the early church. A Jew could not drink milk drawn by Gentiles or eat their food. Jews could not aid a Gentile mother in her hour of need. Jewish physicians could not attend to non-Jewish patients. No Jew would have anything to do with a Gentile. They were unclean.

Unless that Jew, of course, was Jesus. . . . He took an entirely different approach. He was all about including people, not excluding them. "The Word became flesh and made his dwelling among us" (John 1:14). Jesus touched lepers and loved foreigners and spent so much time with party-goers that people called him a "glutton and a drunkard, a friend of tax collectors and sinners" (Matthew 11:19).

Racism couldn't keep him from the Samaritan woman, demons couldn't keep him from the demoniac. His Facebook page included the likes of Zacchaeus the Ponzi-meister, Matthew the IRS agent, and some floozy he met at Simon's house. Jesus spent thirty-three years walking in the mess of this world. "[He], being in very nature God, did not consider equality with God something to be used to his own advantage; rather, he made himself nothing by taking the very nature of a servant, being made in human likeness" (Philippians 2:6–7).

His example sends this message: *no playground displays of superiority.* "Don't call any person common or unfit." . . . In our lifetimes you and I are going to come across some discarded people. Tossed out. Sometimes tossed out by a church. And we get to choose. Neglect or rescue? Label them or love them? We know Jesus' choice. Just look at what he did with us. (From *Outlive Your Life* by Max Lucado.)

# REACTION

**7.** What are some of the ways that Jesus broke through the cultural barriers of his day?

_____

_____

_____

_____

**8.** What example did Jesus set for us in the way he treated people?

_____

_____

_____

_____

**9.** What might have happened if Paul hadn't spoken out against Peter's inconsistent behavior?

_____

_____

_____

_____

**10.** Under what circumstances should you stand up against another leader?

**11.** What are some ways you see modern believers living by rules rather than living by faith?

**12.** How would you respond to a friend who asked, "If salvation is a free gift, and it is based on what Christ has already done for me, why does it matter how I live?"

# LIFE LESSONS

Trying to get right with God by keeping a bunch of religious rules is a formula for frustration and failure. The first problem is . . . *whose rules do we follow?* Such requirements vary from religion to religion, person to person, and generation to generation. What if we're working from the wrong list? This second problem is . . . *how do we define what it means to keep those rules?* Do we have to follow them perfectly? Or are we allowed a reasonable number of mistakes and missteps? And what is considered *reasonable?* The gospel of Christ eliminates all this confusion by stating categorically that no one but Christ is good enough. Only through faith in him, and only by relying on his efforts on our behalf, do we qualify for heaven.

# DEVOTION

*Father, we are not made right with you by human efforts, and we do not stay right with you by works. Remaining "in your good graces" means counting on Christ alone to live in us. Help us to not get caught up in the idea that works = salvation but continue to rely on your grace alone.*

# JOURNALING

What are some legalistic practices that have crept into your life that you need to get rid of?

_____

_____

_____

_____

_____

_____

_____

_____

_____

_____

_____

_____

# FOR FURTHER READING

To complete the book of Galatians during this twelve-part study, read Galatians 2:1–21. For more Bible passages on salvation by grace, read Acts 17:29–31; Romans 5:13–17; Ephesians 2:4–10; 2 Timothy 1:8–10; Titus 2:11–14; and 2 Peter 3:8–10.

# LESSON FOUR

# FAITH ALONE!

*This only I want to learn from you: Did you receive the Spirit by the works of the law, or by the hearing of faith?*
Galatians 3:2 nkjv

# REFLECTION

Faith is one of those words we use a lot but don't demonstrate as we should. Faith should be something we actively *do*. What are the hallmarks of a person who has a living and active faith?

_____

_____

_____

_____

_____

_____

_____

_____

_____

_____

# SITUATION

Paul has now related how God called him to be a minister to the Gentiles and how he received the gospel that he preached to the Galatians. In this next section, he begins to make his defense against the legalistic arguments that his opponents have raised against him. He does this first by admonishing the Galatian believers to recall their own salvation experience and to remember how they found freedom in their new lives in Christ. They had accepted the truth that salvation comes through faith in Christ alone—that religious works, no matter how great, do not merit greater approval from God. Would they now turn their backs on that truth?

# OBSERVATION

*Read Galatians 3:1–9 from the New International*
*Version or the New King James Version.*

NEW INTERNATIONAL VERSION

[1] You foolish Galatians! Who has bewitched you? Before your very eyes Jesus Christ was clearly portrayed as crucified. [2] I would like to learn just one thing from you: Did you receive the Spirit by the works of the law, or by believing what you heard? [3] Are you so foolish? After beginning by means of the Spirit, are you now trying to finish by means of the flesh? [4] Have you experienced so much in vain—if it really was in vain? [5] So again I ask, does God give you his Spirit and work miracles among you by the works of the law, or by your believing what you heard? [6] So also Abraham "believed God, and it was credited to him as righteousness."

[7] Understand, then, that those who have faith are children of Abraham. [8] Scripture foresaw that God would justify the Gentiles by faith, and announced the gospel in advance to Abraham: "All nations will be blessed through you." [9] So those who rely on faith are blessed along with Abraham, the man of faith.

NEW KING JAMES VERSION

[1] O foolish Galatians! Who has bewitched you that you should not obey the truth, before whose eyes Jesus Christ was clearly portrayed among you as crucified? [2] This only I want to learn from you: Did you receive the Spirit by the works of the law, or by the hearing of faith? [3] Are you so foolish? Having begun in the Spirit, are you now being made perfect by the flesh? [4] Have you suffered so many things in vain—if indeed it was in vain?

[5] Therefore He who supplies the Spirit to you and works miracles among you, does He do it by the works of the law, or by the hearing of faith?— [6] just as Abraham "believed God, and it was accounted to him for righteousness." [7] Therefore know that only those who are of faith are

sons of Abraham. [8] And the Scripture, foreseeing that God would justify the Gentiles by faith, preached the gospel to Abraham beforehand, saying, "In you all the nations shall be blessed." [9] So then those who are of faith are blessed with believing Abraham.

# EXPLORATION

**1.** What was Paul's goal in asking the Galatian believers who had "bewitched" them (verse 1)?

_____

_____

_____

**2.** What point is Paul making when he asks the believers to recall how they came to faith?

_____

_____

_____

**3.** What role does the Spirit of God play in a person's conversion and ultimate transformation?

_____

_____

_____

**4.** What are some ways Christians can inhibit the Spirit's work in their lives?

_____

_____

_____

**5.** Paul's opponents have said that believers in Christ must follow the practices of the Old Testament law. Given this, what is Paul's reason for mentioning the Jewish patriarch Abraham?

_____

_____

_____

_____

**6.** Paul distinguishes between a life that is reliant on the Holy Spirit and one that depends largely on human effort. Practically speaking, what is the difference?

_____

_____

_____

_____

# INSPIRATION

The real question is not *how do I get more of the Spirit?* Rather, it is *how can the Spirit have more of me?* We'd expect a Mother Teresa-size answer to that question. Build an orphanage. Memorize Leviticus. Bathe lepers. Stay awake through a dozen Lucado books. *Do this and be filled,* we think.

"Do this on your own and be tired," God corrects. Do you desire God's Spirit? Here is what you do. Ask. "Everyone who asks receives. . . . [You] know how to give good gifts to your children, how much more will your Father in heaven give the Holy Spirit to those who ask Him!" (Luke 11:10, 13 NKJV).

The Spirit fills as prayers flow. Desire to be filled with strength? Of course you do. Then pray, "Lord, I receive your energy. Empowered by your Holy Spirit, I can do all things through Christ, who gives me strength." Welcome the Spirit into every room of your heart.

I did something similar with the air of my air conditioner. As I study in my dining room, cool air surrounds me. Outside the sidewalk sizzles in brick-oven heat. But inside I'm as cool as the other side of the pillow. Why? Two reasons. A compressor sits next to my house. I did not build nor install it. It came with the mortgage. Credit the cool house on a good compressor.

But equally credit the open vents. I did not install the "air makers," but I did open the "air blockers." Cool air fills the house because vents are open. I went from room to room, lowering the levers and releasing the air. The Holy Spirit will fill your life as you do the same: as you, room by room, invite him to flow in.

Try this: before you climb out of bed, mentally escort the Spirit into every room of your house. Before your feet touch the floor, open each vent. Got anger in a bedroom? Unpayable bills on a desk? Conflicts in an office? Need some air in the cellar or a change of atmosphere in the hallways? Invite him to fill each corridor of your life. (From *Come Thirsty* by Max Lucado.)

# REACTION

**7.** What are some ways you can "open the vents" and let the Holy Spirit into your day?

_____

_____

_____

**8.** When was the last time a fellow Christian challenged you to rethink a spiritual idea or practice in your life? What happened as a result?

_____

_____

_____

**9.** How would you define the "means of the flesh" (Galatians 3:3)?

**10.** How can you tell if you have stopped living by faith and started relying on the flesh?

**11.** Why does Paul mention Abraham in verses 6–9? What does Paul say about him?

**12.** Why does Satan work so hard to obscure the gospel? How has he distorted it today?

## LIFE LESSONS

Just like Abraham, we are made right with God by faith alone. And just like Abraham, we are commissioned to bless all nations by sharing and showing the good news of God's forgiveness. God's intention is for us—now forgiven and free—to be bright beacons of hope and life in the world. But when we forget that salvation is by grace, we stop shining. Living in our own strength darkens our hearts and deadens our enthusiasm. What's more, when we fall into the trap of trying to earn

God's approval, we paint a misleading and unattractive picture of what it means to be a child of God. Today, we need to revel in the astonishing good news that we are fully accepted in Christ. We can then spend our lives revealing that amazing grace to others.

# DEVOTION

*Lord, protect us from the foolish belief that we can do anything to warrant your continued approval. Help us to remember the joy of our salvation and the freedom we found in you—and not let the enemy convince us it was in any way through our own efforts. Show us each day how to live freely and fully in the grace of your Spirit.*

# JOURNALING

What are some ways the enemy has tried to "bewitch" when it comes to your faith?

_____

_____

_____

_____

_____

_____

_____

# FOR FURTHER READING

To complete the book of Galatians during this twelve-part study, read Galatians 3:1–9. For more Bible passages on legalism, read Mark 2:23–28; Luke 6:1–11; 13:10–17; John 5:1–15; Acts 15:1–21; 21:17–26; and Romans 10:1–4.

LESSON FIVE

# THE LAW AND
# THE PROMISE

*Christ redeemed us from the curse of the law by
becoming a curse for us . . . so that by faith we
might receive the promise of the Spirit.*
GALATIANS 3:13–14

# REFLECTION

When it comes to faith, some people are extremely serious—almost to the point of being grim. Others take a more breezy and light-hearted approach. The more serious group spends much time looking back (or looking within); the lighthearted folks more commonly look forward. The former tend to err on the side of legalism, the latter on the side of license. Which end of the spectrum do you tend to gravitate toward?

# SITUATION

Paul has been warning the Galatian believers against false teachers who have been urging them to exchange the freedom they experienced in Christ for bondage to the Jewish law. So far, he has asked the Galatians to consider his own story of salvation and reflect on their own experiences as evidence for the new life that Jesus provides. Now, he will seek to combat his opponents' claims by drawing on the Old Testament—the very text they are using—to show how religious rules are incapable of enabling a person to become righteous before God.

# OBSERVATION

*Read Galatians 3:10–18 from the New International*
*Version or the New King James Version.*

## NEW INTERNATIONAL VERSION

[10] For all who rely on the works of the law are under a curse, as it is written: "Cursed is everyone who does not continue to do everything written in the Book of the Law." [11] Clearly no one who relies on the law is justified before God, because "the righteous will live by faith." [12] The law is not based on faith; on the contrary, it says, "The person who does these things will live by them." [13] Christ redeemed us from the curse of the law by becoming a curse for us, for it is written: "Cursed is everyone who is hung on a pole." [14] He redeemed us in order that the blessing given to Abraham might come to the Gentiles through Christ Jesus, so that by faith we might receive the promise of the Spirit.

[15] Brothers and sisters, let me take an example from everyday life. Just as no one can set aside or add to a human covenant that has been duly established, so it is in this case. [16] The promises were spoken to Abraham and to his seed. Scripture does not say "and to seeds," meaning many people, but "and to your seed," meaning one person, who is Christ. [17] What I mean is this: The law, introduced 430 years later, does not set aside the covenant previously established by God and thus do away with the promise. [18] For if the inheritance depends on the law, then it no longer depends on the promise; but God in his grace gave it to Abraham through a promise.

## NEW KING JAMES VERSION

[10] For as many as are of the works of the law are under the curse; for it is written, "Cursed is everyone who does not continue in all things which are written in the book of the law, to do them." [11] But that no one is justified by the law in the sight of God is evident, for "the just shall live by faith." [12] Yet the law is not of faith, but "the man who does them shall live by them."

¹³ Christ has redeemed us from the curse of the law, having become a curse for us (for it is written, "Cursed is everyone who hangs on a tree"), ¹⁴ that the blessing of Abraham might come upon the Gentiles in Christ Jesus, that we might receive the promise of the Spirit through faith.

¹⁵ Brethren, I speak in the manner of men: Though it is only a man's covenant, yet if it is confirmed, no one annuls or adds to it. ¹⁶ Now to Abraham and his Seed were the promises made. He does not say, "And to seeds," as of many, but as of one, "And to your Seed," who is Christ. ¹⁷ And this I say, that the law, which was four hundred and thirty years later, cannot annul the covenant that was confirmed before by God in Christ, that it should make the promise of no effect. ¹⁸ For if the inheritance is of the law, it is no longer of promise; but God gave it to Abraham by promise.

# EXPLORATION

**1.** Why would Paul say that "all who rely on the works of the law" are under a curse (verse 1)?

_____

_____

_____

_____

_____

_____

**2.** What about the person who demonstrates radical devotion to God, lives selflessly, and is never seen doing anything wrong? What does that count for in God's sight (see Romans 3:23)?

_____

_____

_____

_____

**3.** What does it mean that the "righteous will live by faith" (verse 11)?

**4.** Why is no one who relies on the law justified before God?

**5.** How does Paul say that Jesus redeemed people from the curse of the law?

**6.** Some of the false teachers in Galatia were apparently claiming the law given to Moses was the fulfillment of the promise given to Abraham. How does Paul refute that idea?

# INSPIRATION

I became a Christian about the same time I became a Boy Scout and made the assumption that God grades on a merit system. Good Scouts move up. Good people go to heaven. . . .

But some thorny questions surfaced. If God saves good people, how good is "good"? God expects integrity of speech but how much? What is the permitted percentage of exaggeration? Suppose the required score is 80 and I score a 79? How do you know your score?

I sought the advice of a minister. Surely he would help me answer the "how good is good?" question. He did, with one word: *do.* Do better. Do more. Do now. "Do good, and you'll be okay." "Do more, and you'll be saved." "Do right, and you'll be all right."

Do.

Be.

Do. Be. Do.

Do-be-do-be-do.

Familiar with the tune? You might be. Most people embrace the assumption that God saves good people. So be good! Be moral. Be honest. Be decent. Pray the rosary. Keep the Sabbath. Keep your promises. Pray five times a day facing east. Stay sober. Pay taxes. Earn merit badges.

Yet for all the talk about being good, still no one can answer the fundamental question: *What level of good is good enough?* Bizarre. At stake is our eternal destination, yet we are more confident about lasagna recipes than the entrance requirements for heaven.

God has a better idea: "For it is by grace you have been saved, through faith—and this is not from yourselves, it is the gift of God" (Ephesians 2:8). We contribute nothing. Zilch. As opposed to the merit badge of the Scout, salvation of the soul is unearned. A gift. Our merits merit nothing. God's work merits everything.

This was Paul's message to the grace-a-lots. I picture his face red, fists clenched, and blood vessels bulging a river on his neck. "Christ redeemed us from the curse of the law by becoming a curse for us"

(Galatians 3:13). Translation: "Say no to the pyramids and bricks. Say no to the rules and lists. Say no to slavery and performance. Say no to Egypt. Jesus redeemed you." (From *Grace* by Max Lucado.)

# REACTION

**7.** Are you familiar with the do-be-do-be-do tune? How have you played it in your life?

_____

_____

_____

_____

_____

**8.** What is the fundamental problem with the idea you can *do* or *be* enough to earn favor with God? Where does this break down when it comes to trying to measure your good works?

_____

_____

_____

_____

_____

**9.** Paul says that *everyone* is cursed who does not always obey what is written in the law (see also James 2:10). Does this seem fair to you? Why or why not?

_____

_____

_____

_____

**10.** How does the good news of Christ solve these thorny problems of doing or being enough?

_____

_____

_____

**11.** What are some of the spiritual blessings that are yours because Christ chose to accept the penalty of your sins?

_____

_____

_____

**12.** Who are some people in your sphere of influence who believe being right with God depends on their living a good life? How can you help them see the truth of grace?

_____

_____

_____

# LIFE LESSONS

Wouldn't you love to have a visual record of Jesus' meeting with Zacchaeus in Luke 19:1–10? The law-obsessed religious leaders must look on in shock as Jesus befriends a notorious crook. Bent on earning God's approval through their religious efforts, these Pharisees and scribes are harsh and judgmental. They frown a lot. They think they can see, but in truth they are blind. They live in bondage to their own foolish pride. A few feet away Jesus, smiling, invites himself to Zacchaeus' house for dinner. He is disarming and gracious. He offers unconditional freedom from failures of the past and a fresh start. Is there a better picture of life-giving grace? Is there a grimmer illustration of the death that comes through trying to earn God's favor?

# DEVOTION

*Jesus, what a wonderful Savior you are! We thank you for putting yourself under the very curse that was meant for us. We praise you for blessing us with the gracious gift of eternal life. May we share this great promise and hope with all those around us.*

# JOURNALING

In what ways did you feel spiritually "cursed" before experiencing God's grace and understanding Christ's unconditional love for you?

# FOR FURTHER READING

To complete the book of Galatians during this twelve-part study, read Galatians 3:10–18. For more Bible passages on the inability of the law to save us, read Romans 3:19–20; 4:13–25; 8:1–4; Hebrews 3:1–6; 8:7–13; and James 2:8–11.

# THE PURPOSE OF THE LAW

*Therefore the law was our tutor to bring us to Christ, that we might be justified by faith. But after faith has come, we are no longer under a tutor.*

GALATIANS 3:24–25 NKJV

# REFLECTION

We've all had the experience of trying to avoid certain temptations, such as the offer of a fattening dessert, or the urge to constantly check our phones, or just watching television when we know we should be doing something more constructive. Why does it seem that something that's off-limits is often all the more tempting?

_____

_____

_____

_____

# SITUATION

Paul has now convincingly shown that no one who relies on the law can ever find salvation before God and that only Jesus' sacrifice on the cross has the true power to save anyone. He used his opponents' own text (the Old Testament) to base his claims and shown that God's promise spoken to Abraham was fulfilled in Christ. But this begs the question: *If people are not saved by trying to follow God's rules, what was the purpose of those rules in the first place?* Paul now seeks to address this particular issue in the next section of his letter.

# OBSERVATION

*Read Galatians 3:19–29 from the New International Version or the New King James Version.*

NEW INTERNATIONAL VERSION
<sup>19</sup> Why, then, was the law given at all? It was added because of transgressions until the Seed to whom the promise referred had come. The law

was given through angels and entrusted to a mediator. [20] A mediator, however, implies more than one party; but God is one.

[21] Is the law, therefore, opposed to the promises of God? Absolutely not! For if a law had been given that could impart life, then righteousness would certainly have come by the law. [22] But Scripture has locked up everything under the control of sin, so that what was promised, being given through faith in Jesus Christ, might be given to those who believe.

[23] Before the coming of this faith, we were held in custody under the law, locked up until the faith that was to come would be revealed. [24] So the law was our guardian until Christ came that we might be justified by faith. [25] Now that this faith has come, we are no longer under a guardian.

[26] So in Christ Jesus you are all children of God through faith, [27] for all of you who were baptized into Christ have clothed yourselves with Christ. [28] There is neither Jew nor Gentile, neither slave nor free, nor is there male and female, for you are all one in Christ Jesus. [29] If you belong to Christ, then you are Abraham's seed, and heirs according to the promise

## New King James Version

[19] What purpose then does the law serve? It was added because of transgressions, till the Seed should come to whom the promise was made; and it was appointed through angels by the hand of a mediator. [20] Now a mediator does not mediate for one only, but God is one.

[21] Is the law then against the promises of God? Certainly not! For if there had been a law given which could have given life, truly righteousness would have been by the law. [22] But the Scripture has confined all under sin, that the promise by faith in Jesus Christ might be given to those who believe. [23] But before faith came, we were kept under guard by the law, kept for the faith which would afterward be revealed. [24] Therefore the law was our tutor to bring us to Christ, that we might be justified by faith. [25] But after faith has come, we are no longer under a tutor.

[26] For you are all sons of God through faith in Christ Jesus. [27] For as many of you as were baptized into Christ have put on Christ. [28] There is

neither Jew nor Greek, there is neither slave nor free, there is neither male nor female; for you are all one in Christ Jesus. ²⁹ And if you are Christ's, then you are Abraham's seed, and heirs according to the promise.

# EXPLORATION

**1.** Why can't people ever hope to keep God's law perfectly?

_____

_____

_____

**2.** If the law can't save people from their sins, why did God give it?

_____

_____

_____

**3.** Legalism is the belief that following certain rules will make you more acceptable in God's sight. Given the purpose of the law, why is this belief flawed?

_____

_____

_____

**4.** What does Paul mean when he says the law was your "guardian" until you found salvation through faith in Christ?

_____

_____

_____

**5.** Would you say God's law a good thing or a bad thing? Why?

_____

_____

_____

**6.** What positive role does God's law play in your spiritual life?

_____

_____

_____

# INSPIRATION

Remember the good ol' days when credit cards were imprinted by hand? The clerk would take your plastic and place it in the imprint machine, and *rrack-rrack,* the numbers would be registered and the purchase would be made . . .

If the noise didn't get you, the statement at the end of the month would. Thirty days is ample time to *rrack* up enough purchases to *rrack* your budget.

And a lifetime is enough to *rrack* up some major debt in heaven. You yell at your kids, *rrack-rrack.*

You covet a friend's car, *rrack-rrack.*

You envy your neighbor's success, *rrack-rrack.*

You break a promise, *rrack-rrack.*

You lie, *rrack-rrack.*

You lose control, *rrack-rrack . . .*

Further and further in debt.

Initially, we attempt to repay what we owe. . . . Every prayer is a check written, and each good deed is a payment made. If we can do one good act for every bad act, then won't our account balance out in the end? If I can counter my cussing with compliments, my lusts with loyalties, my complaints with contributions, my vices with victories—then won't my account be justified? . . .

There it is. That's the question. How do I deal with the debt I owe to God? Deny it? My conscience won't let me.

Find worse sins in others? God won't fall for that. Claim lineage immunity? Family pride won't help.

Try to pay it off? I could, but that takes us back to the problem. We don't know the cost of sin. We don't even know how much we owe.

Then what do we do? Listen to Paul's answer: "All are justified freely by his grace through the redemption that came by Christ Jesus. God presented Christ as a sacrifice of atonement, through the shedding of his blood—to be received by faith" (Romans 3:24–25).

Simply put: The cost of your sins is more than you can pay. The gift of your God is more than you can imagine. "A person is justified by faith," Paul explains, "apart from the works of the law" (verse 28). (From *In the Grip of Grace* by Max Lucado.)

# REACTION

**7.** How does a credit card statement reveal the amount of debt you owe? How would you apply this analogy to how God's law reveals the debt you owe for your sins?

_____

_____

_____

_____

**8.** What is the problem with trying to pay off spiritual debt by doing good works?

_____

_____

_____

_____

**9.** If the law of God can't bring spiritual life, where does spiritual life begin?

_____

_____

_____

**10.** What would you say is the value in reading and studying the Old Testament?

_____

_____

_____

**11.** How has Christ become your guardian? What does this mean in terms of how you can now approach God (see Hebrews 4:14–16)?

_____

_____

_____

**12.** What does it mean to be "one" with others in Christ Jesus?

_____

_____

_____

# LIFE LESSONS

In the time of Christ, the rule-keeping scribes had dissected and cata-logued the Torah (the first five books of the Bible) into 613 individual commandments—365 "don'ts" and 248 "do's." Also on the scene were assorted rabbis (or teachers) who debated endlessly among themselves about how a God-fearing person was supposed to interpret and apply these divine decrees. Each rabbi had his own spin on things, his own "yoke" or way of understanding the Torah. The result was a confusing, often contradictory, and always exhausting way of life. Enter the rabbi Jesus. He offered a new "yoke" (see Matthew 11:28–30)—a radical new way of life that begins by coming to him (see John 6:35, 37). We make peace with God and enter into real life not when we try hard to be good but when we trust Jesus to give us his righteousness.

# DEVOTION

*Lord Jesus, thank you for giving us freedom in you. We praise you for the stunning fact that we are made right with God by grace and by trusting in your payment for our sins. You have written your law on our hearts and given us your Spirit. Help us to listen to his voice and follow his lead.*

# JOURNALING

How does the fact that all believers are "one in Christ Jesus" affect the way you look at yourself and the way you treat other believers?

# FOR FURTHER READING

To complete the book of Galatians during this twelve-part study, read Galatians 3:19–29. For more Bible passages on the purpose of the law, read Romans 3:19–20; 5:18–21; 7:1–7; Ephesians 2:14–16; 1 Timothy 1:8–11; and Hebrews 7:18–22.

# CHILDREN OF GOD

*So you are no longer a slave, but God's child; and since you are his child, God has made you also an heir.*
GALATIANS 4:7

# REFLECTION

It is common to hear people make comments such as, "Well, it doesn't matter whether you're Christian, Hindu, Muslim, or whatever—the fact is we are *all* God's children." What do you think about this statement? Do you feel it is true, partly true, or not true at all?

_____

_____

_____

_____

_____

_____

_____

_____

_____

_____

_____

# SITUATION

Paul continues in this section of his letter to show how the purpose of the Mosaic Law was to point people to Christ. He does so here by continuing his analogy of how the law formerly served as a "guardian" to people. As long as people were under the law, it was as if they were underaged heirs to their father's inheritance and had to be governed by a trustee. But now, because of Christ, we have reached maturity and can receive our full inheritance. We are God's children, adopted into his family, and can receive all the benefits this status offers.

# OBSERVATION

*Read Galatians 4:1–11 from the New International
Version or the New King James Version.*

NEW INTERNATIONAL VERSION

[1] What I am saying is that as long as an heir is underage, he is no different from a slave, although he owns the whole estate. [2] The heir is subject to guardians and trustees until the time set by his father. [3] So also, when we were underage, we were in slavery under the elemental spiritual forces of the world. [4] But when the set time had fully come, God sent his Son, born of a woman, born under the law, [5] to redeem those under the law, that we might receive adoption to sonship. [6] Because you are his sons, God sent the Spirit of his Son into our hearts, the Spirit who calls out, "Abba, Father." [7] So you are no longer a slave, but God's child; and since you are his child, God has made you also an heir.

[8] Formerly, when you did not know God, you were slaves to those who by nature are not gods. [9] But now that you know God—or rather are known by God—how is it that you are turning back to those weak and miserable forces? Do you wish to be enslaved by them all over again? [10] You are observing special days and months and seasons and years! [11] I fear for you, that somehow I have wasted my efforts on you.

NEW KING JAMES VERSION

[1] Now I say that the heir, as long as he is a child, does not differ at all from a slave, though he is master of all, [2] but is under guardians and stewards until the time appointed by the father. [3] Even so we, when we were children, were in bondage under the elements of the world. [4] But when the fullness of the time had come, God sent forth His Son, born of a woman, born under the law, [5] to redeem those who were under the law, that we might receive the adoption as sons.

[6] And because you are sons, God has sent forth the Spirit of His Son into your hearts, crying out, "Abba, Father!" [7] Therefore you are

no longer a slave but a son, and if a son, then an heir of God through Christ.

⁸ But then, indeed, when you did not know God, you served those which by nature are not gods. ⁹ But now after you have known God, or rather are known by God, how is it that you turn again to the weak and beggarly elements, to which you desire again to be in bondage? ¹⁰ You observe days and months and seasons and years. ¹¹ I am afraid for you, lest I have labored for you in vain.

# EXPLORATION

**1.** What comparison does Paul make between an heir that is underage and a slave? How does he apply this analogy to believers in Christ?

_____

_____

_____

**2.** In what ways did the Mosaic Law serve as a "guardian" and "trustee" to people?

_____

_____

_____

**3.** What does Paul mean when he says, "God sent his Son . . . that we might receive adoption to sonship" (verses 4–5)?

_____

_____

_____

**4.** What are the benefits of being in the family of God?

_____

_____

_____

**5.** As an heir of God, what sort of inheritance do you stand to receive?

_____

_____

_____

**6.** What does Paul say that he fears he has wasted his efforts on the Galatian believers?

_____

_____

_____

# INSPIRATION

God is building a family. A permanent family. Earthly families enjoy short shelf lives. Even those who sidestep divorce are eventually divided by death. God's family, however, will outlive the universe. "For this reason I kneel before the Father, from whom every family in heaven and on earth derives its name" (Ephesians 3:14–15).

Jesus even defined his family according to faith, not flesh. "A multitude was sitting around Him; and they said to Him, 'Look, Your mother and Your brothers are outside seeking You.' But He answered them, saying, 'Who is My mother, or My brothers? . . . Whoever does the will of God is My brother and My sister and mother'" (Mark 3:32–33, 35 NKJV).

Common belief identifies members of God's family. And common affection unites them. Paul gives this relationship rule for the church: "Be kindly affectionate to one another with brotherly love" (Romans 12:10 NKJV). The apostle plays the wordsmith here, bookending the verse with fraternal-twin terms. He begins with _philostorgos_ (_philos_ means friendly; _storgos_ means family love) and concludes with _philadelphia_ (_phileo_ means tender affection; _adelphia_ means brethren).

An awkward but accurate translation of the verse might be, "Have a friend/family devotion to each other in a friend/family sort of way."

If Paul doesn't get us with the first adjective, he catches us with the second. In both he reminds us: the church is God's family.

You didn't pick me. I didn't pick you. You may not like me. I may not like you. But since God picked and likes us both, we are family. And we treat each other as friends. (From *Cure for the Common Life* by Max Lucado.)

# REACTION

**7.** Paul says that because of Jesus, believers in him have been made full heirs in God's family. When has your church or circle of Christian friends felt most like a family?

_____

_____

_____

**8.** How do cultural, racial, and socioeconomic differences make it difficult for Christians to live like a close-knit family?

_____

_____

_____

**9.** What are the benefits of believers viewing themselves as a close-knit family? What kind of message does this send to the outside world?

_____

_____

_____

**10.** What, if anything, needs to change for you to start treating other believers as spiritual siblings and fellow heirs of God?

_____

_____

_____

**11.** Do you address God as your "Father"? Is this a tough concept for you to get your mind and heart around? Why or why not?

**12.** Do you tend to live more like a slave of God's law or more like a child and heir of God?

# LIFE LESSONS

What good parent loves one child more than another? None! However, wise and caring parents will demonstrate their affection to their children in different ways, depending on factors such as personality, age, and life situation. So it is with God. He doesn't deal with his children exactly the same way. Many realities come into play, which is why we should never compare ourselves to others or envy other Christians' relationship with God. Each of our relationships with God will be unique. He will bless us in certain ways and will bless others in different ways. Despite the discrepancies, He loves each of us with perfect and unconditional love. He adores each of us and considers us infinitely special. We are heirs of his endless spiritual blessings!

# DEVOTION

*Father, what a privilege to be your children through faith in Christ. Help us to fully recognize the status you have given to us as the blessings you have provided. Help us to remember we are members of the ultimate royal family and give us the wisdom to live up to that pedigree.*

# JOURNALING

What do you picture when you think of God as your "Father"? Why do you think you feel this way when you view him in that role?

_____

_____

_____

_____

_____

_____

_____

_____

_____

_____

_____

_____

_____

_____

_____

_____

_____

# FOR FURTHER READING

To complete the book of Galatians during this twelve-part study, read Galatians 4:1–11. For more Bible passages on being a part of God's family, read Isaiah 63:15–19; John 1:9–13; Romans 8:14–17; 2 Corinthians 6:14–18; Philippians 2:12–18; and 1 John 3:1–3.

# BECOMING LIKE CHRIST

*My trial which was in my flesh you did not despise or reject, but you received me as an angel of God, even as Christ Jesus.*
GALATIANS 4:14 NKJV

# REFLECTION

As the old saying goes, "You can't teach an old dog new tricks." What do you think about this saying? Do you know any exceptions to the notion that people can't change radically in life?

---

# SITUATION

Paul continues to defend against his opponents' claims that believers in Christ must abide by Jewish customs and regulations by making an impassioned plea to the Galatians to remember the time that they spent together. While it is not clear to what "illness" Paul is referring in this section, what is clear is that the way the Galatians responded has left a warm and lasting impression on the apostle. He calls on the believers to remember this time and not treat him as an enemy for telling them the truth. He pleads with them to continually seek to be transformed, by faith, into the likeness of Christ in their thoughts, character, and actions.

# OBSERVATION

*Read Galatians 4:12–20 from the New International
Version or the New King James Version.*

### NEW INTERNATIONAL VERSION

[12] I plead with you, brothers and sisters, become like me, for I became like you. You did me no wrong. [13] As you know, it was because of an illness that I first preached the gospel to you,[14] and even though my illness was a trial to you, you did not treat me with contempt or scorn. Instead, you welcomed me as if I were an angel of God, as if I were Christ Jesus himself. [15] Where, then, is your blessing of me now? I can testify that, if you could have done so, you would have torn out your eyes and given them to me. [16] Have I now become your enemy by telling you the truth?

[17] Those people are zealous to win you over, but for no good. What they want is to alienate you from us, so that you may have zeal for them. [18] It is fine to be zealous, provided the purpose is good, and to be so always, not just when I am with you. [19] My dear children, for whom I am again in the pains of childbirth until Christ is formed in you, [20] how I wish I could be with you now and change my tone, because I am perplexed about you!

### NEW KING JAMES VERSION

[12] Brethren, I urge you to become like me, for I became like you. You have not injured me at all. [13] You know that because of physical infirmity I preached the gospel to you at the first. [14] And my trial which was in my flesh you did not despise or reject, but you received me as an angel of God, even as Christ Jesus. [15] What then was the blessing you enjoyed? For I bear you witness that, if possible, you would have plucked out your own eyes and given them to me. [16] Have I therefore become your enemy because I tell you the truth?

[17] They zealously court you, but for no good; yes, they want to exclude you, that you may be zealous for them. [18] But it is good to be zealous in a

good thing always, and not only when I am present with you. [19] My little children, for whom I labor in birth again until Christ is formed in you, [20] I would like to be present with you now and to change my tone; for I have doubts about you.

# EXPLORATION

**1.** What does Paul mean when he speaks of becoming like other people (see also 1 Corinthians 9:22)? How is this not being "fake"?

_____

_____

_____

**2.** What was evidently the situation that had brought Paul and the Galatian believers together?

_____

_____

_____

**3.** How had the Galatians treated Paul at that time? How had their attitude since changed?

_____

_____

_____

**4.** How can telling the truth result in changed relationships—either good or bad?

_____

_____

_____

**5.** What does Paul say the false teachers (the so-called "Judaizers") were doing? How was this affecting the relationship between Paul and the Galatian believers?

_____

_____

_____

**6.** What does it mean to have Christ "formed" in us (verse 19)?

_____

_____

_____

# INSPIRATION

When my daughter Jenna was a toddler, I used to take her to a park not far from our apartment. One day as she was playing in a sandbox, an ice-cream salesman approached us. I purchased her a treat, and when I turned to give it to her, I saw her mouth was full of sand. Where I intended to put a delicacy, she had put dirt.

Did I love her with dirt in her mouth? Absolutely. Was she any less my daughter with dirt in her mouth? Of course not. Was I going to allow her to keep the dirt in her mouth? No way. I loved her right where she was, but I refused to leave her there. I carried her over to the water fountain and washed out her mouth. Why? Because I love her.

God does the same for us. He holds us over the fountain. "Spit out the dirt, honey," our Father urges. "I've got something better for you." And so he cleanses us of filth: immorality, dishonesty, prejudice, bitterness, greed. We don't enjoy the cleansing; sometimes we even opt for the dirt over the ice cream. "I can eat dirt if I want to!" we pout and proclaim. Which is true—we can. But if we do, the loss is ours.

God has a better offer. He wants you to be just like Jesus. Isn't that good news? You aren't stuck with today's personality. You aren't condemned to "grumpydom." You are tweakable. Even if you've worried each day of your life, you needn't worry the rest of your life. So what if you were born a bigot? You don't have to die one.

Where did we get the idea we can't change? From whence come statements such as, "It's just my nature to worry," or, "I'll always be pessimistic," or, "I can't help the way I react"? Who says? Would we make similar statements about our bodies? "It's just my nature to have a broken leg. I can't do anything about it." Of course not. If our bodies malfunction, we seek help. Shouldn't we do the same with our hearts? Shouldn't we seek aid for our sour attitudes? Can't we request treatment for our selfish tirades?

Of course we can. Jesus can change our hearts. He wants us to have a heart like his. (From *Just Like Jesus* by Max Lucado.)

# REACTION

**7.** Jesus wants to change each of our hearts. What are the tools he uses to do this?

_____

_____

_____

**8.** Why is this kind of change so difficult?

_____

_____

_____

**9.** What are some ways God corrects his children—to get them to "spit out the dirt" so they can enjoy the "something better" he has for them?

_____

_____

_____

**10.** What forces or obstacles stand in the way of lasting soul transformation?

_____

_____

_____

**11.** What are some areas in your life where you sense God has been trying to bring about deeper transformation?

_____

_____

_____

**12.** How can you be a practical and positive force for change in the lives of those around you this week? Give some specific action steps.

_____

_____

_____

## LIFE LESSONS

The goal of the Christian life is not gaining more knowledge, comprehending a bunch of theology, or memorizing large chunks of the Bible. Following Christ is also not about activity, signing up to serve ceaselessly at church, or tackling a daily to-do list for God. Christ's ultimate desire for each of us is to make us like himself. Once we become God's children by faith in Christ—once we receive a brand-new nature (see 2 Corinthians 5:17)—he wants to utterly transform, from the inside out, the way we think and talk and act. He does this primarily by the truth of his Word, by the power of his Spirit, and with the encouragement of his people. Life is his laboratory for remaking us into the people he originally envisioned before sin plunged the world into darkness and ruin. So take heart, Christian, Christ is being formed in you!

# DEVOTION

*Father, thank you for the astounding promise that you are continually transforming us into the likeness of Christ. We pray that we will cooperate fully with the nudgings and promptings of your Spirit today. Give us eyes that see and a will that yields to your sometimes-painful transforming work.*

# JOURNALING

What are three specific ways in which you would like to become more like Jesus?

---

---

---

---

---

---

---

---

---

---

# FOR FURTHER READING

To complete the book of Galatians during this twelve-part study, read Galatians 4:12–20. For more Bible passages on transformation, read Psalm 51:10–12; Romans 8:26–30; 1 Corinthians 15:44–49; 2 Corinthians 3:12–18; Philippians 3:20–21; and 2 Peter 1:3–9.

# SLAVERY OR FREEDOM?

*We are not slave children, obligated to the Jewish laws, but children of the free woman, acceptable to God because of our faith.*
GALATIANS 4:31 TLB

# REFLECTION

There are so many great stories told in the Old Testament—Noah and the Flood, the Israelites crossing the Red Sea, David battling Goliath. What Old Testament story do you find to be the most spiritually inspiring to you? Why?

---

---

---

---

# SITUATION

So far in Paul's letter to the Galatians, he has made multiple appeals for the believers to remember the freedom they experienced at the time of their salvation and not revert to the bondage of the law that the false teachers are wanting them to adopt. In this section, Paul once again pulls from his opponents' textbook to illustrate the difference between living under the law and living by grace. This time, Paul will cite the story of Sarah and Hagar told in Genesis 16 to illustrate the two covenants—old and new—that God made with his people.

# OBSERVATION

*Read Galatians 4:21–31 from the New International Version or the New King James Version.*

NEW INTERNATIONAL VERSION
[21] Tell me, you who want to be under the law, are you not aware of what the law says? [22] For it is written that Abraham had two sons, one by the

slave woman and the other by the free woman. ²³ His son by the slave woman was born according to the flesh, but his son by the free woman was born as the result of a divine promise.

²⁴ These things are being taken figuratively: The women represent two covenants. One covenant is from Mount Sinai and bears children who are to be slaves: This is Hagar. ²⁵ Now Hagar stands for Mount Sinai in Arabia and corresponds to the present city of Jerusalem, because she is in slavery with her children. ²⁶ But the Jerusalem that is above is free, and she is our mother. ²⁷ For it is written:

> "Be glad, barren woman,
>     you who never bore a child;
> shout for joy and cry aloud,
>     you who were never in labor;
> because more are the children of the desolate woman
>     than of her who has a husband."

²⁸ Now you, brothers and sisters, like Isaac, are children of promise. ²⁹ At that time the son born according to the flesh persecuted the son born by the power of the Spirit. It is the same now. ³⁰ But what does Scripture say? "Get rid of the slave woman and her son, for the slave woman's son will never share in the inheritance with the free woman's son." ³¹ Therefore, brothers and sisters, we are not children of the slave woman, but of the free woman.

## NEW KING JAMES VERSION

²¹ Tell me, you who desire to be under the law, do you not hear the law? ²² For it is written that Abraham had two sons: the one by a bondwoman, the other by a freewoman. ²³ But he *who was* of the bondwoman was born according to the flesh, and he of the freewoman through promise, ²⁴ which things are symbolic. For these are the two covenants: the one from Mount Sinai which gives birth to bondage, which is Hagar— ²⁵ for this Hagar is Mount Sinai in Arabia, and corresponds to Jerusalem

which now is, and is in bondage with her children— ²⁶ but the Jerusalem above is free, which is the mother of us all. ²⁷ For it is written:

> "Rejoice, O barren,
> You who do not bear!
> Break forth and shout,
> You who are not in labor!
> For the desolate has many more children
> Than she who has a husband."

²⁸ Now we, brethren, as Isaac was, are children of promise. ²⁹ But, as he who was born according to the flesh then persecuted him who was born according to the Spirit, even so it is now. ³⁰ Nevertheless what does the Scripture say? "Cast out the bondwoman and her son, for the son of the bondwoman shall not be heir with the son of the freewoman." ³¹ So then, brethren, we are not children of the bondwoman but of the free.

# EXPLORATION

**1.** What are some reasons people often prefer a law-based spirituality?

**2.** What differences does Paul point out between Abraham's two sons?

**3.** What does the son born to Hagar represent? What does the son born to Sarah represent?

**4.** In what ways are believers "children of the promise" like Isaac?

**5.** Sarah told Abraham, "Get rid of that slave woman . . . for that woman's son will never share in the inheritance with my son Isaac" (Genesis 21:10). What is Paul trying to show to the Galatians by citing this verse?

**6.** What does freedom in Christ really mean—in practical and everyday terms?

# INSPIRATION

How would you fill in this blank? *A person is made right with God through*

———.

Simple statement. Yet don't let its brevity fool you. How you complete it is critical; it reflects the nature of your faith. A person is made right with God through . . .

<u>Being good</u>. A person is made right with God through goodness. Pay your taxes. Give sandwiches to the poor. Don't drive too fast or drink too much or drink at all. Christian conduct—that's the secret.

<u>Suffering</u>. There's the answer. That's how to be made right with God—suffer. Sleep on dirt floors. Stalk through dank jungles. Malaria. Poverty. Cold days. Night-long vigils. Vows of chastity. Shaved heads, bare feet. The greater the pain, the greater the saint.

No, no, no. The way to be made right with God? <u>Doctrine</u>. Dead-center interpretation of the truth. Air-tight theology which explains every mystery. The Millennium simplified. Inspiration clarified. The role of women defined once and for all. God has to save us—we know more than he does.

How are we made right with God? All of the above have been tried. All are taught. All are demonstrated. But none are from God. In fact, that is the problem. *None* are from God. All are from people. Think about it. Who is the major force in the above examples? Humankind or God? Who does the saving, you or him?

If we are saved by good works, we don't need God—weekly reminders of the do's and don'ts will get us to heaven. If we are saved by suffering, we certainly don't need God. All we need is a whip and a chain and the gospel of guilt. If we are saved by doctrine, then, for heaven's sake, let's study! We don't need God, we need a lexicon. Weigh the issues. Explore the options. Decipher the truth.

But be careful, student . . . if you are saving yourself, you never know for sure about anything. You never know if you've hurt enough, wept enough, or learned enough. Such is the result of computerized religion:

fear, insecurity, instability. (From *And the Angels Were Silent* by Max Lucado.)

# REACTION

**7.** How have you attempted to "fill in the blank" about what makes a person right with God?

_____

_____

_____

_____

**8.** When was the time in your life that the "lightbulb first came on" and you realized the gospel offers unconditional acceptance and radical freedom?

_____

_____

_____

_____

**9.** What does the miraculous birth of Isaac suggest about the nature of grace?

_____

_____

_____

_____

**10.** What is the best way to respond to people who have a law-based approach to God?

_____

_____

_____

_____

**11.** In your own spiritual experience, do you feel more often like a child of Hagar or like a child of Sarah? Why?

_____

_____

_____

_____

**12.** What are the most common ways you are tempted to fall back into thinking that approval with God is based on your compliance with certain rules?

_____

_____

_____

_____

# LIFE LESSONS

With the glorious freedom offered under God's *new* covenant, why would anyone prefer the *old*? It's a good question with a complex answer. Some don't like grace because it's too wild and risky. Others cringe because it's too vast and hard to measure. Still others bristle because it's "unfair." Really, bad people forgiven? Completely? Without *doing* anything? Opposite of grace stands the law. Hard and fast rules. Concrete formulas. Clear and measurable goals for which a person can strive. The law is a system that caters to human pride by promising to reward the hardest working and most competitive. But the true reward? Bondage, a pervading sense of obligation, fear, and guilt. And—in fine print— the guarantee of ultimate failure. No wonder Paul says, "Therefore no one will be declared righteous in God's sight by the works of the law" (Romans 3:20).

# DEVOTION

*Father, today when we are tormented by the ruthless demands and perfect standards of the law, remind us that we are, by virtue of Christ, free. We are true spiritual children of Abraham and Sarah. Give us the wisdom and strength to cast away all legalistic thoughts.*

# JOURNALING

How is freedom from the law unique to Christianity? How does this challenge you to live differently?

# FOR FURTHER READING

To complete the book of Galatians during this twelve-part study, read Galatians 4:21–31. For more Bible passages on freedom in Christ, read Isaiah 61:1–3; Matthew 11:28–30; John 8:31–36; Romans 6:15–18; Ephesians 2:6–10; and 1 Peter 2:13–16.

# EMANCIPATION!

*It is for freedom that Christ has set us free.*
*Stand firm, then, and do not let yourselves be*
*burdened again by a yoke of slavery.*

GALATIANS 5:1

# REFLECTION

Someone has wisely observed that life is a journey or race. Indeed, these metaphors are found in the Bible to describe what it means to follow Christ. Using this analogy, think of a recent experience in which you got off the path. What derailed you? How did you get back on track?

_____

_____

_____

_____

_____

# SITUATION

Paul continues to defend the gospel he preached to the Galatians—a gospel based on the grace, liberty, and freedom found in Christ—by giving his readers a strong warning. When it comes to living according to the law, it is not a "both-and" proposition but an "either-or" deal. The believers could either _try_ to keep the law perfectly (which, of course, is not possible), or they could acknowledge their need for a Savior. There was no middle ground.

# OBSERVATION

*Read Galatians 5:1–15 from the New International Version or the New King James Version.*

NEW INTERNATIONAL VERSION

¹ It is for freedom that Christ has set us free. Stand firm, then, and do not let yourselves be burdened again by a yoke of slavery.

² Mark my words! I, Paul, tell you that if you let yourselves be circumcised, Christ will be of no value to you at all. ³ Again I declare to

every man who lets himself be circumcised that he is obligated to obey the whole law. ⁴ You who are trying to be justified by the law have been alienated from Christ; you have fallen away from grace. ⁵ For through the Spirit we eagerly await by faith the righteousness for which we hope. ⁶ For in Christ Jesus neither circumcision nor uncircumcision has any value. The only thing that counts is faith expressing itself through love.

⁷ You were running a good race. Who cut in on you to keep you from obeying the truth?⁸ That kind of persuasion does not come from the one who calls you. ⁹ "A little yeast works through the whole batch of dough." ¹⁰ I am confident in the Lord that you will take no other view. The one who is throwing you into confusion, whoever that may be, will have to pay the penalty. ¹¹ Brothers and sisters, if I am still preaching circumcision, why am I still being persecuted? In that case the offense of the cross has been abolished. ¹² As for those agitators, I wish they would go the whole way and emasculate themselves!

¹³ You, my brothers and sisters, were called to be free. But do not use your freedom to indulge the flesh; rather, serve one another humbly in love. ¹⁴ For the entire law is fulfilled in keeping this one command: "Love your neighbor as yourself." ¹⁵ If you bite and devour each other, watch out or you will be destroyed by each other.

## New King James Version

¹ Stand fast therefore in the liberty by which Christ has made us free, and do not be entangled again with a yoke of bondage. ² Indeed I, Paul, say to you that if you become circumcised, Christ will profit you nothing. ³ And I testify again to every man who becomes circumcised that he is a debtor to keep the whole law. ⁴ You have become estranged from Christ, you who attempt to be justified by law; you have fallen from grace. ⁵ For we through the Spirit eagerly wait for the hope of righteousness by faith. ⁶ For in Christ Jesus neither circumcision nor uncircumcision avails anything, but faith working through love.

⁷ You ran well. Who hindered you from obeying the truth? ⁸ This persuasion does not come from Him who calls you. ⁹ A little leaven

leavens the whole lump. $^{10}$ I have confidence in you, in the Lord, that you will have no other mind; but he who troubles you shall bear his judgment, whoever he is.

$^{11}$ And I, brethren, if I still preach circumcision, why do I still suffer persecution? Then the offense of the cross has ceased. $^{12}$ I could wish that those who trouble you would even cut themselves off!

$^{13}$ For you, brethren, have been called to liberty; only do not use liberty as an opportunity for the flesh, but through love serve one another. $^{14}$ For all the law is fulfilled in one word, even in this: "You shall love your neighbor as yourself." $^{15}$ But if you bite and devour one another, beware lest you be consumed by one another!

# EXPLORATION

**1.** Apparently, some of the non-Jewish believers in Galatia were submitting to the Jewish rite of circumcision. Why were they doing this?

_____

_____

_____

_____

**2.** How does attempting to rigidly follow the law indicate you have fallen away from grace?

_____

_____

_____

_____

**3.** What do you think is the point behind religious rituals like baptism and the Lord's Supper?

_____

_____

_____

**4.** What is the only true test for whether our faith pleases God (see verse 6)?

_____

_____

_____

**5.** What does Paul say awaits those who are throwing the Galatian believers into confusion?

_____

_____

_____

**6.** How is the entire law summed up in the command to "love your neighbor as yourself" (verse 14)?

_____

_____

_____

# INSPIRATION

True humility is not thinking lowly of yourself but thinking accurately of yourself. The humble heart does not say, "I can't do anything." Rather, it says, "I can't do everything. I know my part and am happy to do it."

When Paul writes "_value_ others above yourselves" (Philippians 2:3), he uses a verb that means "to calculate" or "to reckon." The word implies a conscious judgment resting on carefully weighed facts. To consider others better than yourself, then, is not to say you have no place; it is to say that you know your place. "Do not think of yourself more highly than you ought, but rather think of yourself with sober judgment, in accordance with the faith God has distributed to each of you" (Romans 12:3). . . .

Again, is Jesus not our example? Content to be known as a carpenter. Happy to be mistaken for the gardener. He served his followers by washing their feet. He serves us by doing the same. Each morning he gifts us with beauty. Each Sunday he calls us to his table. Each moment he dwells in our hearts. And does he not speak of the day when he as "the master will dress himself to serve and tell the servants to sit at the table, and he will serve them" (Luke 12:37 NCV)?

If Jesus is so willing to honor us, can we not do the same for others? Make people a priority. Accept your part in his plan. . . . And, most of all, regard others as more important than yourself. Love does. For love "does not boast, it is not proud" (1 Corinthians 13:4). (From *A Love Worth Giving* by Max Lucado.)

# REACTION

**7.** Why is the simple command to "serve one another humbly with love" (Galatians 5:13) so difficult to live out?

**8.** What does it mean to *value* others above yourself?

**9.** What does it mean to abuse the gift of God's grace?

**10.** What precautions should you to make sure you don't misuse your freedom in Christ?

**11.** How should you look to Jesus' example when seeking to live out your faith?

_____

_____

_____

**12.** Who are three people you will commit to serve this week with love? What will you do?

_____

_____

_____

## LIFE LESSONS

Christian freedom doesn't mean permission to do whatever we want. It means liberation from the prison of self-absorption and from enslavement to insecurity and pride. We grasp that God, in Christ, really does love us and accept us. We realize he lives in us to change us, meet our needs, and touch others through us—and we are changed. We no longer have to strive to get his attention or earn his approval or stay in his good graces. We already enjoy those things to an infinite degree! Suddenly, we are emancipated to turn our focus and attention to the needs of others. We serve them by letting God's divine love flow through us! The secret to a life of freedom? Resting in his perfect grace and relying on his infinite strength.

## DEVOTION

_Lord, open our eyes to the life-changing truth that "the important thing is faith—the kind of faith that works through love" (Galatians 5:6 ncv). Give us hearts to serve others with love._

# JOURNALING

What are the primary ways you've been gifted by God to serve others?

# FOR FURTHER READING

To complete the book of Galatians during this twelve-part study, read Galatians 5:1–15. For more Bible passages on being liberated and called to serve, read Matthew 20:25–28; Mark 10:43–44; Luke 10:25–37; John 13:12–17; Acts 20:18–19; and Philippians 2:1–8.

# FOLLOWING THE SPIRIT

*But the fruit of the Spirit is love, joy, peace, longsuffering, kindness, goodness, faithfulness, gentleness, self-control. Against such there is no law.*
GALATIANS 5:22–23 NKJV

# REFLECTION

Jesus once said you can tell a lot about a person by looking at the "fruit" that his or her life produces (see Matthew 7:15–20). How have you found this to be true in your life?

_____

_____

_____

_____

_____

# SITUATION

Paul has previously outlined what it means to be free in Christ and how believers should use that freedom to humbly serve one another. He now expounds on this idea by first explaining what a person's life will look like if he or she is being led by selfish desires—and the "fruit of the flesh" that such a life will produce. He contrasts this against what a life led by the Spirit will resemble—and the "fruit of the Spirit" that such a life will produce. Paul argues that those who are truly in step with the Holy Spirit will put to death their former ways and bear the kind of fruit that God wants to produce in their lives.

# OBSERVATION

*Read Galatians 5:16–26 from the New International Version or the New King James Version.*

NEW INTERNATIONAL VERSION

<sup>16</sup> So I say, walk by the Spirit, and you will not gratify the desires of the flesh. <sup>17</sup> For the flesh desires what is contrary to the Spirit, and the Spirit

what is contrary to the flesh. They are in conflict with each other, so that you are not to do whatever you want. [18] But if you are led by the Spirit, you are not under the law.

[19] The acts of the flesh are obvious: sexual immorality, impurity and debauchery; [20] idolatry and witchcraft; hatred, discord, jealousy, fits of rage, selfish ambition, dissensions, factions [21] and envy; drunkenness, orgies, and the like. I warn you, as I did before, that those who live like this will not inherit the kingdom of God.

[22] But the fruit of the Spirit is love, joy, peace, forbearance, kindness, goodness, faithfulness, [23] gentleness and self-control. Against such things there is no law. [24] Those who belong to Christ Jesus have crucified the flesh with its passions and desires. [25] Since we live by the Spirit, let us keep in step with the Spirit. [26] Let us not become conceited, provoking and envying each other.

## New King James Version

[16] I say then: Walk in the Spirit, and you shall not fulfill the lust of the flesh. [17] For the flesh lusts against the Spirit, and the Spirit against the flesh; and these are contrary to one another, so that you do not do the things that you wish. [18] But if you are led by the Spirit, you are not under the law.

[19] Now the works of the flesh are evident, which are: adultery, fornication, uncleanness, lewdness, [20] idolatry, sorcery, hatred, contentions, jealousies, outbursts of wrath, selfish ambitions, dissensions, heresies, [21] envy, murders, drunkenness, revelries, and the like; of which I tell you beforehand, just as I also told you in time past, that those who practice such things will not inherit the kingdom of God.

[22] But the fruit of the Spirit is love, joy, peace, longsuffering, kindness, goodness, faithfulness, [23] gentleness, self-control. Against such there is no law. [24] And those who are Christ's have crucified the flesh with its passions and desires. [25] If we live in the Spirit, let us also walk in the Spirit. [26] Let us not become conceited, provoking one another, envying one another.

# EXPLORATION

**1.** How does walking "by the Spirit" keep a person from gratifying "the desires of the flesh" (verse 16)?

**2.** How can a you tell when you are being led by the Spirit?

**3.** What do you make of the fact that Paul lumps selfishness and envy in with "witchcraft" (verse 20) and "adultery" (verse 19 NKJV)?

**4.** What warning does Paul give to those who choose to be led by the flesh?

**5.** What does it mean to crucify "the flesh with its passions and desires" (verse 24)?

**6.** What counsel from this passage would you give to a Christian friend who admitted he or she was having trouble being patient with a coworker?

_____

_____

_____

_____

# INSPIRATION

Most Christians find the cross of Christ easier to accept than the Spirit of Christ. Good Friday makes more sense than Pentecost. Christ, our substitute. Jesus taking our place. The Savior paying for our sins. These are astounding, yet embraceable, concepts. They fall in the arena of transaction and substitution, familiar territory for us. But Holy Spirit discussions lead us into the realm of the supernatural and unseen. We grow quickly quiet and cautious, fearing what we can't see or explain.

It helps to consider the Spirit's work from this angle. What Jesus did in Galilee is what the Holy Spirit does in us. Jesus _dwelt among_ the people, teaching, comforting, and convicting. The Holy Spirit _dwells within_ us, teaching, comforting, and convicting. The preferred New Testament word for this promise is _oikeo_, which means "live or dwell." _Oikeo_ descends from the Greek noun _oikos_, which means "house." The Holy Spirit indwells the believer in the same way a homeowner indwells a house.

"Those who live according to the flesh have their minds set on what the flesh desires; but those who live in accordance with the Spirit have their minds set on what the Spirit desires. . . . You, however, are not in the realm of the flesh but are in the realm of the Spirit, if indeed the Spirit of God lives in you. And if anyone does not have the Spirit of Christ, they do not belong to Christ. But if Christ is in you, then even though your body is subject to death because of sin, the Spirit gives life because of righteousness" (Romans 8:5, 9–10). (From _Come Thirsty_ by Max Lucado.)

# REACTION

**7.** Is it hard for you to grasp the biblical idea that God himself has taken up residence in your life in the person of the Spirit of Christ? Why or why not?

_____

_____

_____

_____

**8.** How does it help you to understand the Holy Spirit's role in your life to consider that he has taken up residence within you like a homeowner "indwells" a house?

_____

_____

_____

_____

**9.** The Spirit of God, when given free rein in your life, will produce various kinds of "fruit" or character qualities. Which of these qualities that Paul lists do you see growing in you?

_____

_____

_____

_____

**10.** Which fruit of the Spirit would you like to yield a greater harvest in your life? Why?

_____

_____

_____

**11.** Paul says to follow or "keep in step" with the Spirit (Galatians 5:25). How can you learn to better hear his voice?

**12.** What spiritual struggles are you battling right now? How are you seeking help from the Holy Spirit to walk in step with him and put the desires of the flesh to death?

## LIFE LESSONS

The Christian life isn't merely difficult; it's impossible. Impossible, that is, so long as we try to live for God in our own strength. Resisting sinful urges? Overcoming our natural tendencies toward pride and selfishness? Serving others in love? Face it, we will *never* do those things until we surrender to the Spirit of God. What a tragic mistake—and a devilish lie—to believe we need the Spirit to begin the Christian life but not to continue living it. Like a strong wind (see John 3:8), or a mighty river (see John 7:38–39), the Holy Spirit longs to move powerfully through our souls. Revealing, convicting, comforting, Counseling, guiding, transforming, empowering. Have you invited him to do his work? Are you yielded fully to his leadership?

## DEVOTION

*Spirit of God, be unleashed in our hearts. Do the work that only you can do to produce the fruit that you desire to see within us. Fall fresh on us. Fill us, mold us, and use us for your purposes. Produce the character of Jesus in our lives.*

# JOURNALING

What steps do you need to take this week to produce more of the fruit of the Spirit in your life?

_____

_____

_____

_____

_____

_____

_____

_____

_____

_____

_____

_____

_____

_____

_____

_____

_____

_____

# FOR FURTHER READING

To complete the book of Galatians during this twelve-part study, read Galatians 5:16–26. For more Bible passages on living in the Spirit, read Joel 2:28–32; Luke 24:44–49; John 6:61–64; 14:16–18; 15:26–27; 16:12–15; Acts 1:7–8; and Romans 8:9–11.

# LESSON TWELVE

# A GRACE-FULL LIFE

*Carry each other's burdens, and in this way you will fulfill the law of Christ.*
GALATIANS 6:2

# REFLECTION

Christians tend to shy away from confronting one another, but the Bible calls us to hold each other accountable. What has been your experience in this area? Have you ever been approached by another believer about your behavior? If so, what happened?

_____

_____

_____

_____

_____

_____

_____

_____

_____

_____

_____

_____

_____

# SITUATION

Paul's concludes his letter to the Galatian churches by showing that when people try to live by the law, it prompts them to compare and complete with others. However, when they embrace grace, it results in becoming a compassionate spiritual family. Paul calls on the believers to test their own actions in this to see what type of "seed" they are sowing—seed that will produce the "fruit of the flesh" or the "fruit of the Spirit." His parting counsel to the Galatians is for them to stop worrying about how others are living and live like the new grace-filled people they are.

# OBSERVATION

*Read Galatians 6:1–18 from the New International Version or the New King James Version.*

### New International Version

[1] Brothers and sisters, if someone is caught in a sin, you who live by the Spirit should restore that person gently. But watch yourselves, or you also may be tempted. [2] Carry each other's burdens, and in this way you will fulfill the law of Christ. [3] If anyone thinks they are something when they are not, they deceive themselves. [4] Each one should test their own actions. Then they can take pride in themselves alone, without comparing themselves to someone else, [5] for each one should carry their own load. [6] Nevertheless, the one who receives instruction in the word should share all good things with their instructor.

[7] Do not be deceived: God cannot be mocked. A man reaps what he sows. [8] Whoever sows to please their flesh, from the flesh will reap destruction; whoever sows to please the Spirit, from the Spirit will reap eternal life. [9] Let us not become weary in doing good, for at the proper time we will reap a harvest if we do not give up. [10] Therefore, as we have opportunity, let us do good to all people, especially to those who belong to the family of believers.

[11] See what large letters I use as I write to you with my own hand!

[12] Those who want to impress people by means of the flesh are trying to compel you to be circumcised. The only reason they do this is to avoid being persecuted for the cross of Christ. [13] Not even those who are circumcised keep the law, yet they want you to be circumcised that they may boast about your circumcision in the flesh. [14] May I never boast except in the cross of our Lord Jesus Christ, through which the world has been crucified to me, and I to the world. [15] Neither circumcision nor uncircumcision means anything; what counts is the new creation. [16] Peace and mercy to all who follow this rule—to the Israel of God.

[17] From now on, let no one cause me trouble, for I bear on my body the marks of Jesus.

[18] The grace of our Lord Jesus Christ be with your spirit, brothers and sisters. Amen.

## New King James Version

[1] Brethren, if a man is overtaken in any trespass, you who are spiritual restore such a one in a spirit of gentleness, considering yourself lest you also be tempted. [2] Bear one another's burdens, and so fulfill the law of Christ. [3] For if anyone thinks himself to be something, when he is nothing, he deceives himself. [4] But let each one examine his own work, and then he will have rejoicing in himself alone, and not in another. [5] For each one shall bear his own load.

[6] Let him who is taught the word share in all good things with him who teaches.

[7] Do not be deceived, God is not mocked; for whatever a man sows, that he will also reap. [8] For he who sows to his flesh will of the flesh reap corruption, but he who sows to the Spirit will of the Spirit reap everlasting life. [9] And let us not grow weary while doing good, for in due season we shall reap if we do not lose heart. [10] Therefore, as we have opportunity, let us do good to all, especially to those who are of the household of faith.

[11] See with what large letters I have written to you with my own hand! [12] As many as desire to make a good showing in the flesh, these would compel you to be circumcised, only that they may not suffer persecution for the cross of Christ. [13] For not even those who are circumcised keep the law, but they desire to have you circumcised that they may boast in your flesh. [14] But God forbid that I should boast except in the cross of our Lord Jesus Christ, by whom the world has been crucified to me, and I to the world. [15] For in Christ Jesus neither circumcision nor uncircumcision avails anything, but a new creation.

[16] And as many as walk according to this rule, peace and mercy be upon them, and upon the Israel of God.

¹⁷ From now on let no one trouble me, for I bear in my body the marks of the Lord Jesus.

¹⁸ Brethren, the grace of our Lord Jesus Christ be with your spirit. Amen.

# EXPLORATION

**1.** What is the right response when a fellow believer succumbs to temptation?

**2.** How can you decide whether it is appropriate to confront another person in love?

**3.** Why is conceit so dangerous? How do people deceive themselves by being conceited?

**4.** How would you describe the spiritual law that "a man reaps what he sows" (verse 7)?

**5.** Why are believers in Christ never to grow weary in doing good?

_____

_____

_____

**6.** What does Paul say are the true motives of those false teachers who want the Galatian believers to adopt Jewish practices like circumcision?

_____

_____

# INSPIRATION

I like the story of the little boy who fell out of bed. When his mom asked him what happened, he answered, "I don't know. I guess I stayed too close to where I got in."

Easy to do the same with our faith. It's tempting just to stay where we got in and never move.

Pick a time in the not-too-distant past. A year or two ago. Now ask yourself a few questions. How does your prayer life today compare with then? How about your giving? Have both the amount and the joy increased? What about your church loyalty? Can you tell you've grown? And Bible study? Are you learning to learn?

"We will _grow_ to become in every respect the mature body of him who is the head, that is, Christ" (Ephesians 4:15).

"Let us move beyond the elementary teachings about Christ and be taken forward to _maturity_" (Hebrews 6:1).

"Like newborn babies, crave pure spiritual milk, so that by it you may _grow up_ in your salvation" (1 Peter 2:2).

"But _grow_ in the grace and knowledge of our Lord and Savior Jesus Christ" (2 Peter 3:18).

Growth is the goal of the Christian. Maturity is mandatory. If a child ceased to develop, the parent would be concerned, right? Doctors would be called. Tests would be run. When a child stops growing, something is wrong.

When a Christian stops growing, help is needed. If you are the same Christian you were a few months ago, be careful. You might be wise to get a checkup. Not on your body, but on your heart. Not a physical, but a spiritual. (From *When God Whispers Your Name* by Max Lucado.)

## REACTION

**7.** Growth, maturity, life change. Whatever you call it, how have you grown in recent years?

_____

_____

_____

**8.** Why is spiritual growth mandatory in the life of a believer in Christ?

_____

_____

_____

**9.** Paul says to "carry each other's burdens" (Galatians 6:2) even as each person "should carry their own load" (verse 5). What is the difference?

_____

_____

_____

**10.** How can you help your brothers and sisters in Christ grow out of a stagnant faith?

_____

_____

_____

**11.** How do you stay motivated to keep loving and serving others—especially on days when you feel like quitting?

_____

_____

_____

**12.** What are some opportunities you have in the next day or so to "do good to all, especially to those who are of the household of faith" (verse 10 NKJV)?

_____

_____

_____

# LIFE LESSONS

Paul sums up his timeless message to the Galatians by saying, "It is not important if a man is circumcised or uncircumcised. The important thing is being the new people God has made" (6:15 NCV). While few believers today struggle with the issue of circumcision, we constantly battle other legalistic pressures. Always there is the temptation to fall back into a rule-keeping mindset—that subtle, insidious way of thinking that says, "I must follow certain religious rules if I want God's approval." To this Paul says, "No! The spiritual life that pleases God (and satisfies our own souls) is being the new creatures that God has made us to be" (see 2 Corinthians 5:17). We live by grace. We grow by following the leading of God's Spirit, who lives in us. True spirituality isn't imposed from without; it bubbles up and overflows from within.

# DEVOTION

_Father, we want so much to know your grace, to revel in it, to be changed by it, and to share it with the world. Keep us from becoming conceited._

*Cause us to realize that the cross of Jesus Christ is the only reason we have for bragging. Thank you, Lord.*

# JOURNALING

Paul concludes by saying, "I have scars on my body that show I belong to Christ Jesus" (verse 17). What evidence do you have from your life that shows you belong to Jesus?

# FOR FURTHER READING

To complete the book of Galatians during this twelve-part study, read Galatians 6:1–18. For more Bible passages on living by grace, read Psalm 84:10–12; Luke 2:39–40; Acts 13:42–43; 2 Corinthians 8:9–12; 12:9–10; James 4:4–7; and 1 Peter 5:5–7.

# LEADER'S GUIDE FOR SMALL GROUPS

Thank you for your willingness to lead a group through *Life Lessons from Galatians*. The rewards of being a leader are different from those of participating, and we hope you find your own walk with Jesus deepened by this experience. During the twelve lessons in this study, you will guide your group through selected passages in Galatians and explore the key themes of the letter. There are several elements in this leader's guide that will help you as you structure your study and reflection time, so be sure to follow along and take advantage of each one.

## BEFORE YOU BEGIN

Before your first meeting, make sure the group members have their own copy of the *Life Lessons from Galatians.* study guide so they can follow along and have their answers written out ahead of time. Alternately, you can hand out the guides at your first meeting and give the group some time to look over the material and ask any preliminary questions. Be sure to send a sheet around the room during that first meeting and have the members write down their name, phone number, and email address so you can keep in touch with them during the week.

There are two ways to structure the duration of the study. You can choose to cover each lesson individually for a total of twelve weeks of discussion, or you can combine two lessons together per week for a total of six weeks of discussion. (Note that if the group members read the selected passages of Scripture for each lesson, they will cover the entire book of Galatians during the study.) The following table illustrates these options:

**Twelve-Week Format**

| Week | Lessons Covered | Reading |
|------|-----------------|---------|
| 1 | Leaving Grace? | Galatians 1:1–10 |
| 2 | Defending the Gospel | Galatians 1:11–24 |
| 3 | Right with God | Galatians 2:1–21 |
| 4 | Faith Alone! | Galatians 3:1–9 |
| 5 | The Law and the Promise | Galatians 3:10–18 |
| 6 | The Purpose of the Law | Galatians 3:19–29 |
| 7 | Children of God | Galatians 4:1–11 |
| 8 | Becoming Like Christ | Galatians 4:12–20 |
| 9 | Slavery or Freedom? | Galatians 4:21–31 |
| 10 | Emancipation! | Galatians 5:1–15 |
| 11 | Following the Spirit | Galatians 5:16–26 |
| 12 | A Grace-Full Life | Galatians 6:1–18 |

**Six-Week Format**

| Week | Lessons Covered | Reading |
|------|-----------------|---------|
| 1 | Leaving Grace? / Defending the Gospel | Galatians 1:1–24 |
| 2 | Right with God / Faith Alone! | Galatians 2:1–3:9 |
| 3 | The Law and the Promise / The Purpose of the Law | Galatians 3:10–29 |
| 4 | Children of God / Becoming Like Christ | Galatians 4:1–20 |
| 5 | Slavery or Freedom? / Emancipation | Galatians 4:21–5:15 |
| 6 | Following the Spirit / A Grace-Full Life | Galatians 5:16–6:18 |

Generally, the ideal size you will want for the group is between eight to ten people, which ensures everyone will have enough time to participate in discussions. If you have more people, you might want to break up the main group into smaller subgroups. Encourage those who show up at the first meeting to commit to attending the duration of the study, as this will help the group members get to know each other, create stability for the group, and help you know how to prepare each week.

Each of the lessons begins with a brief reflection that highlights the theme you will be discussing that week. As you begin your group time, have the group members briefly respond to the opening question to get them thinking about the topic at hand. Some people may want to tell a long story in response to one of these questions, but the goal is to keep the answers brief. Ideally, you want everyone in the group to get a chance to answer, so try to keep the responses to just a few minutes. If you have more talkative group members, say up front that everyone needs to limit his or her answer to two minutes.

Give the group members a chance to answer, but tell them to feel free to pass if they wish. With the rest of the study, it's generally not a good idea to have everyone answer every question—a free-flowing discussion is more desirable. But with the opening reflection question, you can go around the circle. Encourage shy people to share, but don't force them.

Before your first meeting, let the group members know how the lessons are broken down. During your group discussion time the members will be drawing on the answers they wrote to the Exploration and Reaction sections, so encourage them to always complete these ahead of time. Also, invite them to bring any questions and insights they uncovered while reading to your next meeting, especially if they had a breakthrough moment or if they didn't understand something they read.

# WEEKLY PREPARATION

As the leader, there are a few things you should do to prepare for each meeting:

- *Read through the lesson.* This will help you to become familiar with the content and know how to structure the discussion times.
- *Decide which questions you want to discuss.* Depending on how you structure your group time, you may not be able to cover every

question. So select the questions ahead of time that you absolutely want the group to explore.

- *Be familiar with the questions you want to discuss.* When the group meets you'll be watching the clock, so you want to make sure you are familiar with the Bible study questions you have selected. You can then spend time in the passage again when the group meets. In this way, you'll ensure you have the passage more deeply in your mind than your group members.

- *Pray for your group.* Pray for your group members throughout the week and ask God to lead them as they study his Word.

- *Bring extra supplies to your meeting.* The members should bring their own pens for writing notes, but it's a good idea to have extras available for those who forget. You may also want to bring paper and additional Bibles.

Note that in many cases there will not be one "right" answer to the question. Answers will vary, especially when the group members are being asked to share their personal experiences.

## STRUCTURING THE DISCUSSION TIME

You will need to determine with your group how long you want to meet each week so you can plan your time accordingly. Generally, most groups like to meet for either sixty minutes or ninety minutes, so you could use one of the following schedules:

| Section | 60 Minutes | 90 Minutes |
|---|---|---|
| WELCOME (members arrive and get settled) | 5 minutes | 10 minutes |
| REFLECTION (discuss the opening question for the lesson) | 10 minutes | 15 minutes |
| DISCUSSION (discuss the Bible study questions in the Exploration and Reaction sections) | 35 minutes | 50 minutes |
| PRAYER/CLOSING (pray together as a group and dismiss) | 10 minutes | 15 minutes |

As the group leader, it is up to you to keep track of the time and keep things moving along according to your schedule. You might want to set a timer for each segment so both you and the group members know when your time is up. (Note that there are some good phone apps for timers that play a gentle chime or other pleasant sound instead of a disruptive noise.) Don't feel pressured to cover every question you have selected if the group has a good discussion going. Again, it's not necessary to go around the circle and make everyone share.

Don't be concerned if the group members are silent or slow to share. People are often quiet when they are pulling together their ideas, and this might be a new experience for them. Just ask a question and let it hang in the air until someone shares. You can then say, "Thank you. What about others? What came to you when you reflected on the passage?"

# GROUP DYNAMICS

Leading a group through *Life Lessons from Galatians* will prove to be highly rewarding both to you and your group members—but that doesn't mean you will not encounter any challenges along the way! Discussions can get off track. Group members may not be sensitive to the needs and ideas of others. Some might worry they will be expected to talk about matters that make them feel awkward. Others may express comments that result in disagreements. To help ease this strain on you and the group, consider the following ground rules:

- When someone raises a question or comment that is off the main topic, suggest you deal with it another time, or, if you feel led to go in that direction, let the group know you will be spending some time discussing it.
- If someone asks a question you don't know how to answer, admit it and move on. At your discretion, feel free to invite group members to comment on questions that call for personal experience.

- If you find one or two people are dominating the discussion time, direct a few questions to others in the group. Outside the main group time, ask the more dominating members to help you draw out the quieter ones. Work to make them a part of the solution instead of the problem.

- When a disagreement occurs, encourage the group members to process the matter in love. Encourage those on opposite sides to restate what they heard the other side say about the matter, and then invite each side to evaluate if that perception is accurate. Lead the group in examining other Scriptures related to the topic and look for common ground.

When any of these issues arise, encourage your group members to follow the words from the Bible: "Love one another" (John 13:34), "If it is possible, as far as it depends on you, live at peace with everyone" (Romans 12:18), and, "Be quick to listen, slow to speak and slow to become angry" (James 1:19).

Thank you again for taking the time to lead your group. May God reward your efforts and dedication and make your time together in this study fruitful for his kingdom.

# ALSO AVAILABLE IN THE LIFE LESSONS SERIES

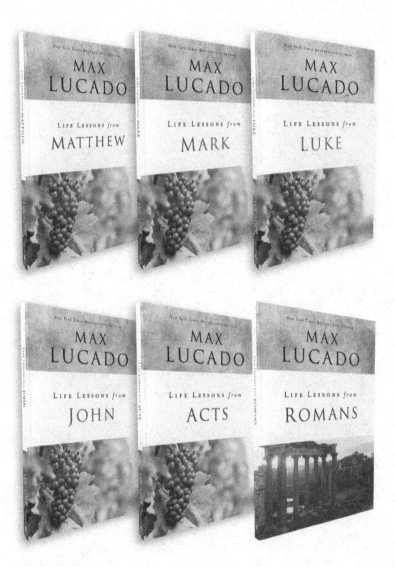

*Now available wherever books and ebooks are sold.*